Boyd Codding...
HOW TO PAINT YOUR
HOT ROD

Timothy Remus

MBI Publishing Company

First published in 1994 by MBI Publishing Company, PO Box 1, 729 Prospect Avenue, Osceola, WI 54020-0001 USA

The information in this book is true and complete to the best of our knowledge. All recommendations are made without any guarantee on the part of the author or Publisher, who also disclaim any liability incurred in connection with the use of this data or specific details.

We recognize that some words, model names and designations, for example, mentioned herein are the property of the trademark holder. We use them for identification purposes only. This is not an official publication.

MBI Publishing Company books are also available at discounts in bulk quantity for industrial or sales-promotional use. For details write to Special Sales Manager at Motorbooks International Wholesalers & Distributors, 729 Prospect Avenue, PO Box 1, Osceola, WI 54020-0001 USA.

Library of Congress Cataloging-in-Publication Data
Remus, Timothy.
    Boyd Coddington's how to paint your hot rod/
    Timothy Remus.
        p. cm.
    Includes bibliographical references.
    ISBN 0-87938-942-7
    1. Hot rods--Painting. I. Coddington, Boyd.
II. Title. III. Title: How to paint your hot rod.
TL255.2.R46   1994
629.228--dc20   94-23273

On the front cover: A close-up of the flamed fender of Gary Lorenzini's "Too Hot Coupe." *Timothy Remus*

Printed in the United States of America

Contents

Introduction

This is a how-to paint book for people painting their hot rods and street rods, cars and trucks that get extra attention to detail when you do a paint job because a great look and an extra nice finish are desired.

This book is meant to help amateur and first-time painters do a great paint job at home on their own vehicle.

Custom painting seems at first like a very daunting task to tackle in the home shop. Somehow, the idea of preparing, masking, and spraying a nice candy paint job seems like more than most of us can handle.

Under the magnifying glass, however, painting turns out to be another of those big jobs that can be broken down into a series of smaller jobs. By themselves, the smaller jobs don't seem so intimidating. This philosophy of taking a big project and making it manageable by breaking it down into a group of smaller projects isn't anything new. Yet, I think we often forget this "big jobs are just a bunch of small jobs" philosophy and allow ourselves to be intimidated.

This book breaks the process of painting down into components. Though this is not a bodywork book, there is a chapter on surface preparation and the use of body filler. There are chapters on the shop and shop tools, understanding modern paints, and surface preparation. More important, or at least more interesting, is the actual how-to-paint information. (For thorough bodywork coverage, check out another book in this series, *Boyd Coddington's How to Build Hot Rod Bodywork*.)

As much as possible, I've presented the real how-to information in a "hands-on" fashion. That is, I take the reader into a respected shop where we follow the project along step by step. I've tried to find the best people I could and then record exactly what they do, how they do it, and why. To help convey the information, the book contains as many photographs as possible.

As much as possible, I tried to create a direct connection between the expert and the reader—to structure the book so that Jon Kosmoski or Doug Thompson can speak directly to the reader.

Though not all readers will want to tackle a flame job or do their own pinstripes, there is information here for anyone who does, from choosing the right materials to the actual layouts. Paint is often applied to more than bodies. In fact, it seems each year more and more people are carefully painting the entire engine and the frame to match. Frame welds are ground and then covered with filler before being sprayed with all the care and attention that hot rod bodies got just a few years ago. If a smooth and polished frame is what you've got to have, then turn to chapter 9 and follow along as Pete and Jake work their magic on a new street rod chassis.

Conclusion

Ultimately, the book is just one more tool to be combined with the spray gun and your own abilities to create a paint job that you can point to with pride and call your own.

Chapter 1

Planning: The Importance of Thinking Before You Shoot

This planning step might seem unnecessary. After all, why should you waste your time planning something as simple as a paint job when that time could be better spent doing the actual work? The reasons for planning are twofold: First, if you think first and act second, you're more likely to get a better paint job. Once the body and metalwork are done, it's too easy to just jump in and start spraying. The trouble comes later

The paint job you choose needs to be more than sexy and more than well applied. It must "fit" the car. The long, flowing flames on Barry Larson's latest Deuce fit the car perfectly. Rodder's Digest

when you realize that for the same amount of work you could have had a better paint job, or one with a more appropriate color.

The second reason for thinking first and painting second is money. Even if you do all your own work, a quality paint job is an expensive undertaking. Urethane paints are expensive; lacquer isn't exactly cheap. Neither are the two-part primers, the plastic body filler, or the spot filler. As long as you're going to spend all those bucks, you should probably make damned sure that the end result is what you had in mind. The only way to do that is to carefully plan the whole job.

Where to Start

This book assumes that the metalwork is finished and the final mud work or skim coat (or whatever you want to call it) is done or nearly done. The paint job is the most visible single thing you're going to do to the car. The success of many great cars owes a lot to the paint job.

Old-timey hot rods, trucks (and of course, Henry J's) look great in suede paint. Remember, though, that primer doesn't seal like a finish paint, so if you intend to leave it suede, use a black or gray with flattener in it and not a true primer.

Scallops have been around for a long time. The long skinny scallops seen on this Ford convertible make it look longer and lower—probably not a bad thing for one of these very round cars. Rodder's Digest

You need to decide on a color or colors, a style, and the need for any graphics, flames, or pinstripes. You must determine not only what color, but what type of paint to use (candy or a straight color, with or without a clearcoat), and what brand of paint to use.

The color and pinstriping used on your car are essential parts of the design for the car. Black primer looks great on an old-time Model A with a flat-motor. On an otherwise perfect smoothie, however, it just makes the

car look unfinished. When it comes to picking a color or design for the paint, remember that fads may leave town faster than the bad guy in a Clint Eastwood movie. More than one hot rodder has repainted a car to get rid of the designs he was so proud of only one or two years before.

Some colors hide a less-than-perfect body while others exaggerate the slightest ripple. There's a good reason why certain hot rodders like suede cars; they are really forgiving, and don't make less-than-perfect bodywork as obvious as some paints do. The darker and shinier the paint, the better the bodywork needs to be because the more apparent any bodywork flaws will be.

Designing the Right Paint Job for Your Car

In the book, *Boyd Coddington's How To Build Hot Rod Bodywork*, you will find a discussion of the pros and cons of using an outside designer. If you went to the trouble to have someone draw up your car, then have them provide suggestions for the paint and pinstripes as well. If you're doing this whole project yourself, then you may need to look at your file of "cars I like" to decide which color you like best and why. Your file should consist of magazine photos of cars whose paint jobs you've admired, and photos you've shot at shows of cars whose looks you liked. If there are elements of several cars' paint jobs that appeal to you, give thought to combining these touches to create the ideal paint scheme for your car. Though it seems obvious, remember that the car is a whole design and the paint is a major part of that design. Don't paint it red because you really like red—unless red happens to be a great color for that new coupe.

Hopefully you spent some time with photos or copy machine copies of your car (or a similar car) trying different top chops or a section job done with scissors and

This very slick '33/'34 Ford carries a very slick, very nineties kind of paint job. The whole thing—the car, its style and the paint—all need to work together.

glue. Get some colored markers and start "painting" those designs done on the copy machine. Your choice of colors is limited to the colors in your marker selection, but at least you can look at the same car in four colors in a matter of minutes.

If you need to see the color on a surface bigger than a paint chip, then bite the bullet and buy a small can of that color and spray some on an old panel lying around the shop. Doug Thompson, a professional car painter and builder, uses old light bulbs. He paints a series of bulbs in different colors and then carries the bulbs around into different lighting situations to see how they look. The curved shape of the bulbs helps him to see how the highlights are going to look.

Though graphics seem to come and go, there is one type of graphic that never goes out of style. That graphic

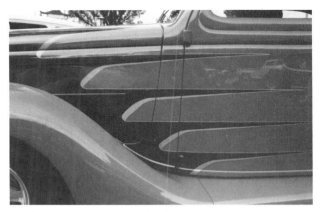

Shadows can be used to add color to a scallop job or to make the scallops stand out more—just one more design decision.

Ya want 'em subtle or ya want 'em LOUD? And do you want them to contrast or complement the overall color? And how many colors should you use? The pinstriper or painter who lays out the flames can help with some of these decisions.

is, of course, flames. Done in white, yellow, and red on an old primered hot rod, they look perfect. More modern flames with overlapping licks done in greens and blues might be just the thing for a smoothed and molded '48 Chevy. Like a good rock-and-roll song, flames never seem to get dated or go out of style.

Which Paint?

Deciding which type and brand of paint to use will depend to some degree on how complex a paint job you want and how much money you've got to spend. Consider that a candy or pearl paint job requires at least three separate painting steps: basecoat, candy-coat, and clearcoat, and that a candy job is hard to "spot-in" if you crunch a fender later.

A straight color, or a color with a clearcoat, is much easier for the first-time painter to apply because it presents less chance for screw-ups, and is easy to spot-in later. Some of the new OEM paints provide the best of both worlds, providing a pearl effect, for example, in a one-step paint.

As the complexity of the paint job goes up, so does the price. Be sure to check the prices of all the materials you intend to buy—the final figure might be a shocker. When possible, buy everything from one manufacturer or supplier (more on this later). That will minimize the chance of lifting or other problems caused by the use of incompatible materials.

Black hot rods look great, but only if the body work under the paint is near-perfect, as is the case with this Ford convertible.
Rodder's Digest

Laying out a set of flames over louvers is a very time consuming proposition and not something that all layout or pinstripe artists enjoy.

Simple, early style coupes call for simple, early style flames.

Before deciding to use the newest, most durable catalyzed urethanes, remember that their use requires a fresh-air hood, while lacquer can be sprayed at home with only a standard charcoal-type of respirator (more on safety later).

What All This Means

The planning step is just an exercise, an exercise designed to make you think about your project. Too many of us paint our cars and automatically choose the same color as our friend's car or one we saw in a magazine. Like a Monday-morning quarterback, it's only after the job is finished that we realize the car would look a lot better in some other color or with a slightly different design.

You need a color that works for the car. You also need a type of paint that makes sense for both you (the painter) and the car, purchased from a reputable paint dealer or jobber who can provide some advice on use of the various products.

This paint job is like everything else, which is to say that it will probably require more work and cost more money than you originally thought. So make it all worthwhile by carefully planning the job.

Interview: Greg Morrell From Boyd's

Greg Morrell has been called Boyd Coddington's "Top Gun." As painter for Boyd for some years now, and for Fat Jack's before that, Greg has a lot of information to offer about paint, painting, and hot rods.

Greg, how about some background: Where did you work before starting work at Boyd's?

I've been at Boyd's for seven years. I took autobody class, graduated in '68. Before working here, I was at Jack's Enterprises (Fat Jack's). Before that I worked at a dealership. In high school I painted a car for my cousin and did some stuff like that. Boyd's, of course, is way off the end. They say you can't make custom work pay, but Boyd's operation just gets bigger and bigger. We do motorcycle parts, paint Mercedes; we do a lot of stuff besides just street rods and hot rods.

Let's talk about painting. When it comes to preparation, what do people miss?

Generally, people get in a hurry when they block sand or sand in the doorjambs. They finger sand without a sanding block. You can't get a car straight that way. Your fingers make grooves in the filler or the primer-surfacer. If you don't use a block your fingers put grooves in the paint. If you want something flat you've got to use something flat to sand with.

You always emphasize the importance of getting the panels flat... It sounds obvious, but can you expand on that?

Well, you can go overboard and sand a bunch of flat ridges into a panel, but I'd rather do that and then have to come back and sand off the tops of the ridges than to do the opposite. I think it's better to get something flat, even if it's almost too flat, than to try to get it flat with the soft pad or no pad so the paper follows the contours. People often do exactly that when they do color sanding; they get in there with 1,500 or 1,000 grit, and they sand the tops off everything, but pretty soon they're just following the orange peel. It doesn't keep sanding flat. I've done cars that someone else painted, and I started color sanding with the 400 grit, then went to 600, and then started polishing (this is a car with a lot of urethane clear on it). I guide coated the whole thing with a dark guide coat before I started.

Do people go too far with the fine papers? Do they go to too fine a grade of paper?

It depends on the situation. If you're doing a pearl or fine metallic, you have to use a pretty fine paper (500 or 600, for example) because that type of paint will show fine sand scratches. But some of our lacquer paint jobs are block sanded with 320 grit before the actual finish painting starts. The coarser paper also helps the paint to really stick. Lacquer softens any old paint you're painting over, and that helps the paint to adhere. Everything here gets done with 320 or 360 grit, unless it's a fine metallic, and then you need something finer to avoid any sand scratches showing through. When you use a sealer, it fills the 320 scratches just fine and then the topcoat will stick to the sealer.

Body men and books are always talking about sand scratch swelling. Is it still a problem, and is it caused by not waiting long enough between coats so the solvents soak down into the layers of filler underneath?

It was a problem when we were using lacquer primer. The solvents in the paint could soak down into the filler and cause it to swell, which made the scratches much worse. With the new two-part materials it isn't such a problem. Sand scratches aren't so much of a problem now; you still have the scratches, but you don't get the swelling.

What about color choice for a particular car?

As far as what color a car should be, it depends a lot on the shape of the body. The Aluma Coupe and Roadstar, they were both originally planned to be red. Well, those cars don't have much shape to speak of except the roundness. So if you paint them in a solid color, they flatten out, you lose a lot of the detail, there's nothing there to catch and reflect the light. We ended up painting them in pearls and metallics. Roadstar, in particular, really shows that double roll in the body because of the metallic.

In bare metal it looks kind of heavy; the paint highlights the double roll in the lower body, which stretches the car out, and I think makes it look a lot better. There are plenty of nice cars painted the wrong color. Everyone has an opinion, but sometimes the color can make or break the car.

In the paint shop, we manipulate reflections. If the car is not straight, then it looks like hell because the light won't flow down the side of the car. On CheZoom there's an S bend at the back of the door, like a cowl on a '32 Ford. If that S curve isn't perfectly smooth, it just looks really bad.

You guys still use a lot of lacquer don't you?

On the Boyd Red, yes. Otherwise we're using more and more urethanes. There's a Toyota Supra Red, which I think is a basecoat-clearcoat system, and that's a really nice red, so we may be using more and more of that.

The Boyd Red, as you spray it today, what color is it really?

The colors that Boyd Red is made out of are translucent; it's almost a candy color. You can see through a 1/2in of it. It's sprayed over a yellow base. You're seeing the yellow through the red, even though you might not realize it.

We've been using a yellow sealer, then two or three coats of the yellow lacquer on top of that, then a minimum of fifteen coats of the red lacquer. And we don't clearcoat the red. Because if you rub through the clear, you can see it. So I only use clear on candies or metallics where they were designed to be clearcoated.

Are there differences between when you paint lacquer and when you paint urethane?

Urethane is a matter of knowing how much to flow out without having it run. People used to shoot lacquer real dry and apply plenty of coats, so there wasn't so much solvent and so much of a chance that the solvent would soak down into the fillers underneath. But that isn't so much of a problem now because there's catalyzed primer under the lacquer (and they won't swell), so I try to spray the lacquer fairly wet. You might want to spray lacquer metallics drier so the metallic will even out—it depends on the situation.

Do you use the new HVLP (high volume low pressure) guns?

Yes, especially for primer and for basecoat-clearcoat jobs. They're kind of like transistor radios, the

longer they make them, the better and cheaper they get. We paid quite a lot for the first one or two guns we bought. And it's hard to use a new piece of equipment when you know the old one works just fine. We're trying to stay as legal as possible.

But, I think painters in general are hard headed; I know I am. We're not always willing to accept new ideas and products. It's sometimes hard to accept new equipment or materials when you've been using something else successfully for a number of years.

When I did Roadstar I used the old high-pressure equipment because it's hard to paint candy on tubing (the chassis tubing); you've got to shoot each tube from about four directions. Three coats of gold, three coats of orange pearl, three coats of candy color, and then a couple of coats of clear. That's so much work, and it's so hard to spray all that tubing that I used my old, trusty high-pressure gun.

How do you set up your high-pressure gun?

Well, it depends on the gun and the situation. Not all high-pressure guns are the same, and not all HVLP guns are the same. Jon Kosmoski recommends that with a regular gun you turn the fan all the way open and then set the fluid until you get a 4in fan and then paint quickly with a 75 percent overlap. It works good
continued on next page

with a candy color because you're misting it on and moving quickly. So again, I adjust the gun depending on the situation, the paint, and the gun.

I only use one or two guns; some guys have a whole bunch of guns, one for clear, one for primer, one for basecoat. It gets to be real expensive. I just use one or two and clean them real good when I change paints or colors.

Is there anything really unique about painting a hot rod?

Well, the reason it takes us two months to paint a car that some bodyshops would do in two days is because we take the whole process a lot further. We carefully finish the doorjambs and the edges of the metal, and we're really careful to make sure the panels are flat.

Do you always bury your graphics under clearcoats?

Generally we do. It's hard with cars (easier with motorcycles), because it adds up to a lot of clearcoat, a lot of expensive material.

Do you always polish the clearcoat, or do you sometimes leave it alone if the clear comes out without any dust or imperfections?

Yes, we almost always do [polish it]; you get a better shine, and you eliminate any orange peel. If the finish is really nice, you could probably skip it, but we usu-ally do buff the clearcoat.

If you were going to pinpoint one or two mistakes that people make when they paint hot rods and high-end jobs, what would they be?

They shouldn't mix brands and materials. We had trouble with lacquer thinners recently; we used two different thinners with the same paint for a particular car, and the car came out with two slightly different colors. And once when Keith and I both cleared a car, with different clear, you could see the difference in the finished paint. People have to use the thinner or reducer that's recommended for a particular product. And people shouldn't assume that the instructions for one brand of urethane basecoat are the same as someone else's. When all else fails, as the old saying goes, read the directions and the tech sheets.

We are real careful to get all the paint at one time, so it's the same batch number and the same color, and we usually mix it all together in one big pail before we start shooting.

Any other comments?

Well, with the cost of the new materials, it's really important to think about what you're doing before you do it, so you don't make any mistakes. It's not just the idea that if you screw up you've got the labor of repainting the car. The cost of materials is so high that if you have to repaint, the cost of paint makes it a real expensive operation.

Chapter 2

The Shop: Make It Safe, Make It Work

You can't overhaul engines without at least a small shop and a certain minimum amount of equipment. Paint and bodywork likewise require that you have (or have access to) a shop and equipment. Even though some of your friends might have elaborate shops with plenty of space and a whole rack of Snap-On tools, the essentials for painting are pretty minimal.

Equipping a Basic Shop

A one-stall garage is the minimum space required. No matter how big it is, the work area must be well lit with good ventilation. You need compressed air (more later), heat (if you live in the north country), and plenty of electrical outlets. The shop needs a floor that can be kept clean; access to running water is a nice bonus.

Remember that while you need ventilation, you also need dust control during those periods when you're spraying paint. An easy way to provide ventilation of a garage is to open the door about 1ft, and use some Dustlok filter material (made by Fiberbond Air Filtration Products) stretched across that opening. At the end of the door, slide in a ventilation fan pushing air out of the shop. Air drawn in will thus pass through the filter, and any dust carried in the air will be trapped in the filter material.

The fan you use to push air out of the shop should be one designed specifically for that job, a fan that runs without any sparks at the brushes and no chance to ignite the flammable fumes often present in a paint shop.

The flammability question affects your choice of heat for the shop, too. If you're lucky enough to live in Southern California, then you may not need to heat the shop at all.

If you require heat, either put the heat source in another room and duct the heat in, use a nonflame heat source like electric baseboard (though there's probably a spark as the thermostat cycles on and off), or simply shut the heater off during times when fumes are present. Remember that gas and solvent fumes are usually heavier than air, so they fall to the floor. This means that if there are any flames or pilot lights or sparks in the shop, you must keep them as high off the floor as possible.

A large, commercial 5hp compressor like this one may seem like too much for a small shop. Yet most spray gun manufacturers recommend that you use a 3hp compressor as minimum, and prefer that you use 5hp. This system uses copper distribution pipe.

15

The point is, you need to be able to heat the shop up to a nice steady 70deg minimum, hopefully without too much humidity and without an open flame. (Thrifty hot-rodders often use wood heat for their garages, though it may not be a good idea when the building is filled with gasoline and flammable chemicals). A lot of paint jobs have been ruined because the paint was applied at just 60deg, or the heat was shut off after the paint was applied and the shop cooled off—so the paint never cured correctly.

Shop Tools

At the heart of the shop is the compressor, the one tool that drives so many others. The size of the air compressor you choose will depend to some extent on the type of paint gun you use (more on guns later). When it comes to buying air compressors, the old adage "bigger is better" definitely applies. The trouble, of course, is that air compressors don't come cheap. The tendency is to wait until a 2 horsepower (hp) model goes on sale at Sears and then proudly drag that shiny new unit home.

Most paint manufacturers recommend you use a compressor with a minimum of 3hp; some think that minimum figure should be 5hp. Jon Kosmoski, owner of House of Kolor and painter for more than thirty years, feels that a high percentage of the painting troubles encountered in small paint shops are caused by insufficient compressor capacity. When looking at the cubic feet per minute (CFM) requirements of spray guns and shop equipment, you can use the guide of 4CFM per horsepower, so a 3hp compressor usually puts out about 12CFM.

Both the equipment you buy and the compressor you use to run that equipment carry a CFM rating. Pay close attention to these ratings when you shop for equipment.

When you consider buying a compressor, consider that the harder it works, the hotter it gets. Soon the air coming out of the compressor heats up, too, carrying a lot of moisture along with it. In the air hose, near the gun, the air cools and the moisture condenses out of the air stream. It only takes one little spit of water to ruin an otherwise perfect paint job. Hot, overworked compressors also pick up more oil from the compressor's crankcase and pass that along with the hot air in the airstream.

If you haven't purchased a compressor yet, save your money and buy a big one. If your compressor isn't big enough, or you don't yet own one, why not rent one for the first paint job? Renting will leave you with more money to spend on the job itself, so the budget doesn't get shot just equipping the shop.

In terms of power tools, you probably already have some grinders and sanders. Professional metal workers like Steve Davis advise against using large, 9in grinders: "People should stay away from those big body grinders; it's probably one of the worst tools that was ever introduced to the body trade. It wants to go in there and cut grooves in the material, and it adds a lot of heat. It also work-hardens the metal."

It's better to use a small grinder when necessary.

A "mud hog" is a common power tool used for shaping filler. Actually a large, air-powered D-A, this tool is usually used with 36 or 80 grit paper and a foam pad. The speed of the disc can be kept low with the trigger so the operator can see more easily how the material is coming along. A smaller D-A is handy for a variety of sanding operations.

In Search of The Holy Grail—A Clean Air Supply

So you bite the bullet and buy a big, killer compressor that looks like it belongs in the back room of the Chevy garage, and you figure your air supply troubles are over. Not exactly. You need more than just a high quantity of air; you also need quality air—air that is clean and dry.

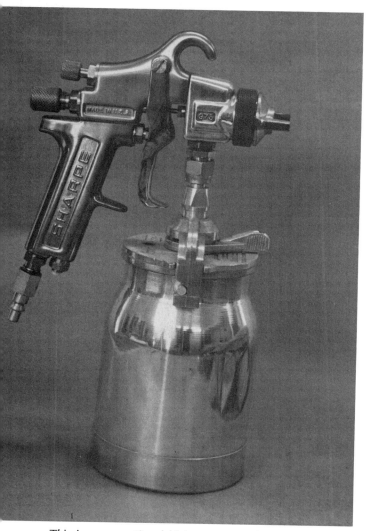

This is a conventional high-pressure siphon type gun from Sharpe. Guns like this have been used successfully for decades, though they operate at a much lower efficiency than the new HVLP equipment.

16

Specifically, you need to run the air through lines with enough capacity to prevent a drop in pressure. In addition to being big enough, the air lines must be routed to discourage the passing of impurities from the main line to the feeder tubes. You also want to avoid big temperature changes in the air lines (as happens when long hoses lay on the garage floor) causing any moisture to condense out of the air stream.

It seems like overkill, yet the air supply is what carries the paint (in most cases). If the air supply is loaded with moisture and impurities, those impurities will show up in your finished paint job.

Starting at the compressor, you need a flexible hose connecting it to the main feeder line. This will isolate the compressor's vibration so it doesn't cause cracks in the main feed line. The main feed line should be at least 3/4in in diameter; the pipe should be either galvanized or copper. Like the compressor, a bigger main feed line is better than a small one. A bigger feed line will handle more air and effectively adds to the size of the compressor's storage tank. The main line should run downhill slightly, with a valve or clean-out at the far end.

It's of note to mention that it would be nice if we could run plastic pipe for the air distribution system because it's so much easier to cut and assemble. The record on plastic pipe, however, is mixed—I have heard horror stories of exploding plastic pipe and also the tale of two commercial shops in Kansas City that have used plastic pipe safely and successfully for a number of years. The key seems to be using the right pipe with a high enough pressure rating and being sure to isolate it from the vibrations of the compressor.

No matter what the material is, the branch lines off the main feeder line should run up and then turn and run down (check the illustration to relieve any confusion), as this will prevent any crud inside the main line from finding its way into the individual lines.

Keeping water out of your air supply involves more than just a large compressor and well designed air lines. Moisture traps are available in a number of designs and should be part of your air distribution system. These traps are available in a variety of styles, from simple little canisters that collect water in the bottom, to large stainless steel containers that hold a quart of water and incorporate a pressure regulator into the design.

There are two important things about these water traps. The most important thing is that you buy and install one, no matter which style you choose. The other important thing about water traps is their location. Most of us mount the trap right next to the compressor; it always seemed like a logical location to me. The trouble is that the air leaving the compressor is hot, so any moisture will exist as a gas—fully absorbed by the air stream. A trap mounted farther along the main feeder tube will be able to trap much more water because the air at that point will have cooled, condensing the water out of the air stream so it will collect in the trap.

There are a few more tips as to this compressor business, and I recommend that you read the *PPG Refinish*

Manual (a great book you can probably obtain from your paint jobber). Now that you've got the expensive compressor, keep the oil clean, just like in your hot rod. When you service the compressor, be sure to keep the intake air filter clean. You might even want to mount the intake outside the building; this will reduce the noise and keep the filter cleaner for a much longer period. Finally, be sure to drain the tank on the air compressor on a regular basis.

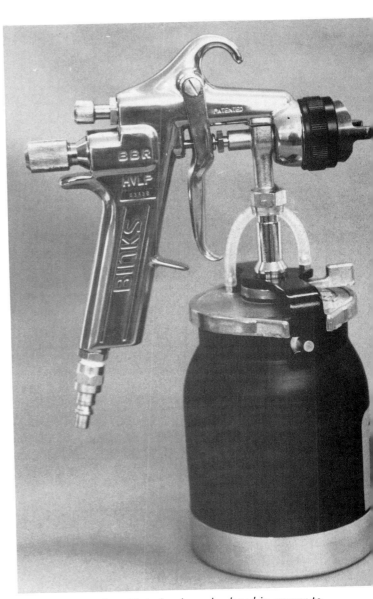

This HVLP gun from Binks has been developed in answer to regulations requiring that spray painting equipment meet improved transfer efficiencies—so a higher percentage of the paint actually goes on the car instead of up into the atmosphere. These guns put approximately three times as much material on the object being painted as the old high-pressure guns.

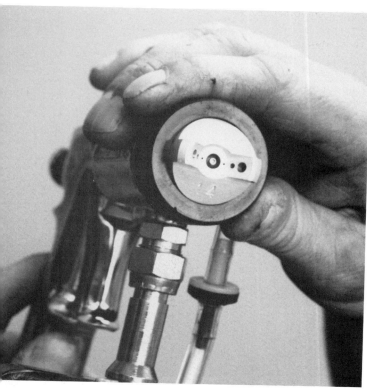

A spray gun, any spray gun, atomizes the paint in two or three stages as the paint leaves the nozzle and mixes with the air. The small holes in the "horns" help to further atomize the paint, though their primary purpose is to shape the paint fan.

Most spray guns have two adjustments—material and fan shape. This high-pressure gun from Sharpe has the adjustments in the "classic" locations: the upper knob controls air to the horns, and thus the shape of the fan. The lower knob controls the amount of material, by controlling the trigger pull.

Spray Guns

Choosing a spray gun used to be a relatively simple matter of matching your budget to the available supply. Once purchased, it was just a matter of learning to use the gun and always keeping it clean. Like a lot of things around us, the world of spray painting—and painting guns in particular—has changed in the last few years.

Today there are two types of spray guns: the standard siphon (or, high-pressure gun) and the newer HVLP (high volume low pressure). The first effective spray gun was developed by a man named DeVilbiss during our Civil War. DeVilbiss discovered that a high-pressure stream of air passing through a tube would siphon liquid from a cup connected to the main air line by a smaller tube. These first spray guns were used to spray medicines and disinfectants during the war, though it was soon found that other liquids could be atomized and applied in this same fashion.

Of note, nonproduction (sometimes called light-duty) spray guns put out less material, but their CFM requirements are much lower than a big production gun. These guns are often well suited to situations where you aren't painting large objects and the compressor size is marginal.

High-pressure Siphon-type Gun

The siphon-type paint gun idea is more than 100 years old. The new guns manufactured by companies like DeVilbiss, Binks, Sharpe, and a dozen more are far superior to anything Mr. DeVilbiss conceived of during the war, yet they are still siphon guns, with all the advantages and disadvantages of that basic design.

On the plus side of the ledger, the high-speed air stream (usually 40 pounds per square inch [psi] or more) does a good job of atomizing the paint and delivering it to the object being painted. On the minus side, however, that high-speed air stream moves the paint at high speed toward—but not always onto—the object being sprayed. Some of the paint misses the object entirely; some of it hits with such force that it bounces back off into the air. Siphon-style guns get as little as 25 percent of the paint on the car. The rest of the paint, as well as the solvents mixed with the paint, go up in the air or on the walls of your shop.

The paint industry has a means of measuring the amount of material that actually goes on the fender, as opposed to the amount that goes up in the atmosphere. Transfer efficiency (TE) is simply a measure of the amount that is actually transferred from the gun to the object. As stated, siphon-style guns commonly have a transfer efficiency of only about 25 percent. By contrast, the new HVLP guns have efficiencies of 65 percent and more.

The modern high-pressure, siphon-type guns feature the same basic design as the guns invented more than a century ago: Essentially, air passing through the spray gun siphons paint from the can that is usually incorporated into the design of the gun. The two-stage trigger controls both air and liquid—pulling the trigger back part way allows air to pass through the gun, while pulling it back all the way allows liquid paint to be pulled from the cup. That liquid paint is introduced to the air stream at the point where the air is leaving the gun.

Paint and air both leave the gun at the air cap and immediately begin to mix. Atomization occurs in two or three stages, beginning when the fluid leaves the gun, surrounded by a column of air that leaves the gun from the ring surrounding the fluid nozzle tip. Most air caps have at least one more set of air ports near the fluid nozzle tip that provide additional air to the paint and air mixture as it leaves the gun. These additional ports provide secondary atomization. Most guns have small air ports in the "horns" of the air cap. These are used primarily to shape the paint; mist though the additional air serves to aid atomization of the paint as well.

Most spray guns of the type we describe have two basic adjustments, the two small knobs commonly seen on the back of the gun. The top knob controls air to the horns of the air cap and thus is used to control the size of the fan. The lower knob controls the material, or the amount of fluid leaving the gun.

Before adjusting the gun to spray a nice pattern, you must choose the right air cap and fluid nozzle. Different materials require the use of different air caps and fluid nozzles and each set has a different CFM rating. Be sure to match the cap and fluid nozzle to both the material you are spraying and the capacity of your compressor.

If you're considering the purchase of a siphon (or high-pressure) gun, consider a nonproduction (sometimes called light-duty) spray gun. These guns put out less material than the production gun, but their CFM requirements are likewise much lower than they are for a production gun. These guns are well suited to situations where you aren't painting large objects (or those large objects are painted one piece at a time) and the compressor size is marginal.

When it comes to setting the adjustments on a new high-pressure gun, each painter seems to have his or her own formula. Professional painter Mallard Teal of St. Paul, Minnesota, uses the basic adjustments they taught him in trade school: "I screw both the material and fan adjustments all the way in and then back out the top [or fan] adjustment three turns and the bottom [material] adjustment three and a half turns." Painter and paint supplier Jon Kosmoski follows a similar procedure, though he uses different adjustment settings. Jon uses the gun with the top adjustment wide open and the material knob backed out about two turns.

There are a few basic points that everyone agrees on when it comes to using a spray gun:

• Try to follow the pressure recommendations set by the paint manufacturer.

• Try to use the lowest pressure that will give the pattern you desire. Ultimately, the correct pressure is the one that gives you the pattern you want.

• One more thing: Gun manufacturers (both high-pressure and HVLP) report that nearly all the complaints they receive can be traced to dirty equipment—so always keep the equipment clean.

HVLP Guns

With an HVLP delivering roughly three times as much material to the object, the amount of paint used is dramatically reduced. This means lower material costs for painting, less overspray in the atmosphere (and on the walls of the shop), and less solvent usage, meaning

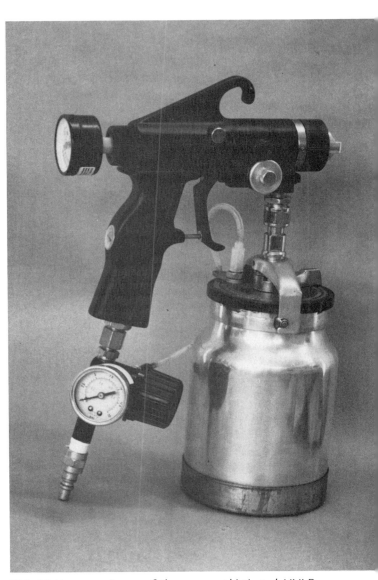

This Mattson gun is one of the more sophisticated HVLP guns on the market. The upper pressure gauge measures air at the air cap, which never exceeds 10psi with a good HVLP gun. The pressure at the air cap is controlled by controlling line pressure. The lower gauge and knob on the Mattson gun allow the user to control the air to the paint cup—thus controlling how much paint is delivered to the air stream. This control can be used to fine tune the finish of paints of different viscosities.

reduced volatile organic compounds (VOC) in the atmosphere.

Southern California has some of the worst air pollution in the world, and the California South Coast Air Quality Management District came up with rule 1151. The rule requires spray guns to meet minimum TE specifications as a means of limiting the amount of VOCs spewed into the air by bodyshops in the region. So far, the only guns to meet the strict standards are the HVLP designs.

HVLP guns come in two basic styles, with a few variations. HVLP guns and systems atomize the paint with a high volume of low-pressure air instead of the standard high-pressure siphon-type gun, where a small volume of high-pressure air is used to atomize the paint. The two basic types of HVLP are turbine-style and compressor-style.

Turbine systems use their own turbine-type compressor to supply a large volume of air to the gun at a low (less than 10psi) pressure. Like most HVLP systems, these systems atomize and carry the paint with a high volume

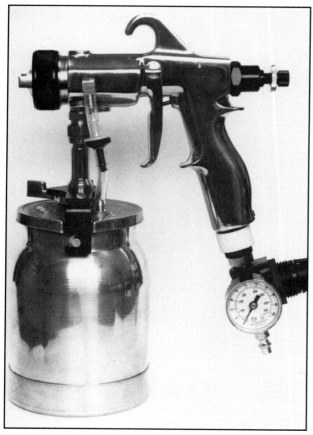

This Croix Air Gun (now owned by Graco) has no adjustment for cup pressure and uses the lower gauge and knob to regulate line pressure. The upper knob on this gun controls material while the shape of the fan is adjusted by moving the air cap.

of low-pressure air. The turbine systems have a number of advantages: By separating the paint gun from the shop's compressor it doesn't matter whether that compressor is 5hp or only 1hp. Also, the high-speed turbine blades tend to heat the air through rotational friction. This heated air expands in the turbine, thus reducing the relative humidity.

Because the turbine doesn't do much compressing, the air stays at a uniform temperature, so problems with condensation in the air lines are minimized. Gone, too, are worries about the compressor picking up oil or contaminants from its own crankcase.

Though turbine systems have advantages, they also have some serious disadvantages. First, these systems add another piece of equipment—the turbine—to an already crowded shop. Second, the pressure of the air leaving the gun tends to be on the low side, even for HVLP-type equipment. As we move into an era of high-solids paints designed for low VOCs, we also move into an era when the viscosity of the paint we are spraying becomes heavier. Turbine systems work great for spraying lacquer or other light-viscosity liquids but often have trouble providing enough air to properly atomize primer-surfacers and low-VOC urethanes.

After some initial failures (which gave all early HVLP equipment a bad name) there are finally some good HVLP guns that run off compressor air. These guns are able to convert the high-pressure compressor air to a low-pressure air—with more volume, of course—inside the gun. The air leaving the gun measures less than 10psi. Unlike siphon guns, most of these guns pressurize the paint in the pot and use that pressure to bring the paint up to meet the air stream.

HVLP guns that run off the shop's compressor come from a variety of suppliers in a wide range of styles. Most require at least a 5hp compressor to ensure an adequate air supply, though as always there are exceptions. Croix Air (now part of Graco Inc.) produces an HVLP gun that uses a venturi in the handle so the air passing through the gun creates a low-pressure area where ambient shop air can be pulled in and added to the air supply moving through the gun—thus reducing the compressor requirements. Mattson, a small midwestern company with a reputation for high-quality HVLP equipment, has a new air-miser air cap designed to bring compressor requirements down into the 9 to 12CFM range (or 3 to 5hp) for most painting situations.

HVLP guns are very similar to the high-pressure siphon guns in their basic anatomy. A one- or two-stage trigger controls fluid and usually the air flow as well. Most have a material control knob like a high-pressure gun, though not all have the conventional "fan control" knob like a high-pressure gun. Some control the fan by moving the air cap or with a small knob built into the gun near the air cap. Most of these guns, whether operated by a turbine or a compressor, apply pressure to the paint in the paint pot.

The Mattson brand of guns have a few unique features that make them more flexible, if slightly more complex to understand at first. Instead of just pressurizing the paint in the cup to the same pressure as that at the air cap, these guns allow the painter to adjust both pressure on the paint in the cup and pressure at the air cap. In the case of a heavy material for example, higher cup pressure can be used to bring the material up to meet the air flow, and then air cap pressure can be set for the best atomization or finish. The other nice feature is a fan control that increases the amount of material in proportion with the fan size you choose. Reduce the fan size, and the amount of material is reduced as well.

As is the case with high-pressure guns, the first step with your new HVLP system is to install the right air cap and fluid nozzle for the material at hand.

Buying an HVLP gun or system isn't the cheapest way to go. For example, the Eastwood catalog offers their Accuspray HVLP turbine system for almost $700 (at the time of printing), while in another section of the same catalog a Binks standard spray gun is $145 plus the price of a cup. They also offer an HVLP gun that runs off shop air for $449. These are neither the highest nor lowest costs for good spray equipment; they are representative of the prices and price differences you will find when shopping for equipment.

It might be tough to justify the extra expense of an HVLP system when a high-pressure siphon gun is so much less costly. On the other hand, keeping the environment clean is a great concept and the new HVLP equipment is already required in many parts of the county. Yet as an occasional painter, you still might not want to spend three times as much money based on that criteria alone.

The HVLP equipment makes more sense when you consider the high cost of material (urethane paints can run as much as $150 per gallon) and the fact that an HVLP system will use a lot less paint. The other major consideration is the mess and fog created by siphon guns in a small shop. Working in your garage, there's never as much ventilation as you'd like and there's usually way more fog in the air than is healthy, even with the right mask and filters. Most HVLP systems will create less than half the overspray, meaning less chance to breathe the often toxic fumes, and less cleanup in the shop afterward.

How to Spray Paint—In Ten Words or Less

When you decide to fire up that paint gun for the first time, you need to remember the basics of spray painting. First, the gun must be moving when you pull the trigger and begin applying material. With a two-stage trigger, painters usually pull the trigger part way so air moves through the gun, start their hand moving, and then fully pull the trigger as the gun approaches the area where they need to start applying paint.

Second, always keep the gun pointed at a 90deg angle to the object being painted. That way the paint goes on evenly. If the gun is tipped relative to the object, then the top or bottom of the paint fan will contain more paint than the other.

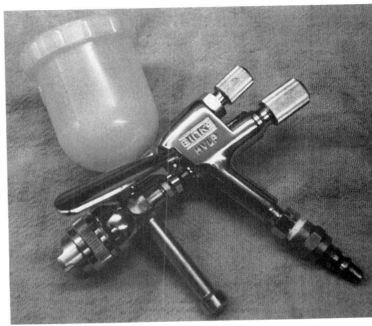

Small touch-up guns are handy for smaller jobs or restricted areas. This neat little gun is a gravity feed, HVLP touch-up gun from Binks, one with fan shape and material controls in the "classic" locations.

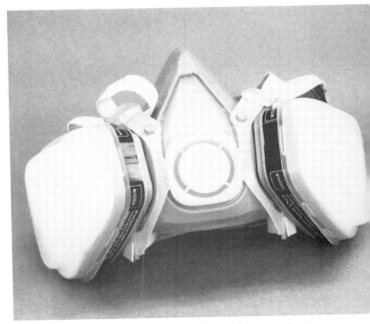

Anytime you paint, you need either a charcoal type respirator like that shown, or a fresh air hood. Charcoal respirators are often used for non-isocyanate paints, though there are exceptions. Some companies, including PPG, recommend fresh air hoods for many of their products that do not contain isocyanates (you need to read the labels and safety sheets). Also, a painter with a beard cannot expect these masks to seal correctly and therefore must use a fresh air hood for all painting.

Third, always move the gun in straight lines across the object. As Jon Kosmoski explains it, "Painters have to draw imaginary straight lines or a grid over the object and follow those with the gun. You can't let each pass across a door or quarter panel turn down and converge at the back of the panel. You have to imagine those straight lines."

An object that combines flat panels with curves (think of a rectangular one-gallon can of lacquer thinner) will require that the flat panels be painted in a series of horizontal passes, combined with a "banding" pass up or down the curved corner.

Forth, unless the paint manufacturer tells you otherwise, each pass of the gun (as you work across a flat pan-el for example) should overlap the last pass by 50 percent.

Shop Safety

Safety is the dullest part of most technical books and the one section too many people skip over. The following comments regarding your safety in the shop have been kept short—in the hope that more readers will actually read them instead of skipping to the next chapter for some "real" information.

We tend to poo-poo safety warnings in the belief that we're too tough or that it can't happen here. The new miracle paints are better than ever, but part of the miracle has been achieved at considerable cost—cost in the form of high toxicity. Whether you only paint once a year or once a week, the chemicals can and will hurt you if you don't take the proper precautions.

The materials you need protection from include dust, paint, and solvent in both vapor and liquid form, and the isocyanate-based materials in both liquid and vapor form.

To protect yourself from sanding dust, always wear at least a good dust filter and eye protection during any work in the shop. You need eye protection, either in the form of goggles or a full-face respirator that includes eye protection into the design of the respirator. The goggles will protect your eyes from flying debris from the grinder, and also prevent vapors from being absorbed by the mucous membranes around your eyes.

A charcoal-type respirator should be used in all painting operations that do not involve isocyanates. Remember that the charcoal will only actively filter the incoming air for a limited amount of time, so always keep the unused filters in a tight plastic bag or coffee can—and don't be cheap; replace the filters on a regular basis. Many painters wear special coveralls and rubber gloves during any painting operations. It protects the wearer from having the chemicals enter through the skin. The coveralls also prevent your flannel shirt from contributing lint to the new paint job.

For spraying urethanes or any paints containing the dread isocyanates—especially in an area where the ventilation is poor, an area other than a paint booth—you need a hood or mask supplied with fresh air from its own compressor. Be sure the air intake for this compressor is outside the paint area. This equipment can be rented from many large rental companies so you don't have to pay out the bucks on equipment that only gets occasional use.

Don't use solvents and thinners to wash your hands or remove paint from hands and arms. Chemicals in the liquids are absorbed through the skin and end up in your blood stream, so always use waterless hand cleaner or a similar product.

Finally, when you're spending hundreds of dollars outfitting your garage, spend just a few more and buy at least one good fire extinguisher designed for gasoline and solvents (the new Halon extinguishers are nice and neat) and a smoke detector.

Paints catalyzed with isocyanates, as well as some other painting products, require the painter to use a pressurized fresh air hood and a complete painter's suit. The fresh air hood requires its own fresh air supply, drawn from outside the painting area.

Interview: Ross Mattson

Ross Mattson is a man intimately familiar with spray painting and spray painting equipment. It was Ross' late father, Roy, who developed the Mattson HVLP gun, but before that, Roy and Ross developed a custom painting system for their own line of motorcycle luggage. Their system of custom paint allowed them to match the factory paint for nearly any modern motorcycle. The system worked so well that it was eventually sold to PPG, where it became the Radiance II custom paint line.

Today Ross oversees the production of the Mattson gun and also runs the two-day training seminars held at the Rice Lake, Wisconsin, plant. Ross Mattson is a man with a lot to say, not just about HVLP equipment, but about spray painting in general.

Ross, maybe you can provide some background on yourself and how you became acquainted with painting and with spray equipment.

We were using conventional spray equipment to paint our own motorcycle luggage (in 1976). That was working very well. Then as our business grew, we went from one shift to three shifts. Because we were spraying around the clock, we began to pollute the environment, to the point that we were knocking on our neighbor's doors with our fumes. And the neighbors came over and complained. We knew we had to change. We didn't know what kind of equipment we would end up with, but something had to change. It's the oldest cliche in the world, but necessity is the mother of invention. We tried all the American- and foreign-made HVLP equipment we could find. Of course HVLP is not a new idea; I mean, the vacuum cleaner systems are HVLP.

The theory has been there for a long time but never really perfected for professional use. So by using and altering the existing equipment that we found, we fell in love with the idea of HVLP. We saw a lot of promise with this type of equipment, but we couldn't find anything that would work on a day-to-day basis. If we were going to grow and prosper we would have to make some changes, and that's what we've always been able to do with Roy (Ross' father and longtime inventor, Roy Mattson). Whenever Dad got involved, problems got solved and people were impressed. So basically, he began to alter existing HVLP equipment. This was all turbine-powered equipment, and eventually we even designed our own industrial turbine system.

A turbine is a turbine, whether it's a vacuum cleaner or not. It's just a high volume of air at low pressure. If you look at why the turbine systems aren't so popular today, it's because of the maintenance of the bearings, the electrical hazard of having this piece of equipment near the spray area, and the fact that turbines don't have as much pressure as you really need. They have the necessary volume but not the PSI. In those days people were spraying a lot of lighter materials: stains, varnishes, lacquer paints, products that were light in viscosity.

The woodworking industry is still a hold-out for the turbine-style equipment. Turbines have guaranteed dry, warm air. It works really well with lacquer-type materials. But now, as we see people going away from lacquer-based paints and even lacquers, the turbine-style systems don't work as well.

We even had a turbine system where we hooked two turbines in tandem in order to get greater PSI. This gave us more like 6 or 7psi and all the volume in the world. That would work pretty well for most paints.

But if we were going to go forward with the whole idea of HVLP, we felt we had to get away from the extra expense, maintenance, cumbersome appearance, and physical size of the turbine. Basically that led us up to the point where we are today with what we call the "direct-connect gun"—one that runs off the shop compressor. We feel the smallest compressor that should be used is 5hp. There are some special air caps that allow a hobbyist to run the gun off a 3hp compressor, but it's not as fast. It can't be used to paint a 45ft trailer.

How do you explain HVLP and what makes it different?

HVLP means high volume, low pressure. When I explain it I try to separate it from conventional equipment. Take a Binks number seven for example, a gun that all professional painters are familiar with. The CFM requirement for the Binks is 12-16cfm, and the pressure at the air cap is about 35lb.

One of our HVLP guns might need anywhere from 8-16cfm, depending on the air cap that you use. But the pressure at the air cap is 10lb or less. So the paint is atomized and carried by a large volume of air leaving the gun at a much lower pressure. By carrying the paint with a lower pressure stream of air, a much higher percentage of the paint that leaves the gun actually strikes, and sticks to, the surface being painted.

What do you see as the main advantage to HVLP spray equipment?

The key point, without a doubt, is the ability of HVLP to save paint. Good equipment saves you money; poor equipment costs you money. By getting more of the paint on the car and creating less overspray, HVLP equipment pays for itself in paint savings. The transfer efficiency of a conventional high-pressure gun might be 30 percent or less. That's the amount of paint that actually stays on the vehicle. Thirty percent is probably generous. What we see in tests is 15-20 percent. You're really spraying with overspray. So 70 percent (usually more) is just going up into the air or on the floor or into your filters or lungs.

continued on next page

If I can show someone that we can do the production that a painter needs and still save at least 20 percent of the paint bill for a bodyshop, that's a lot of money.

There have to be some disadvantages to HVLP.

Yes, the biggest disadvantage is the cost of the equipment, even our least expensive gun is $400. A traditional high-pressure gun is around $200. The other disadvantage is you've got to stand still long enough to learn the variables of low-pressure spraying, because it's not very forgiving. If the gun isn't set up correctly, you will definitely suffer.

We do a lot of training to try to overcome the problems with people using the equipment they don't understand.

You have to understand the theory of spraying with HVLP. You're spraying with a pressurized paint cup. With a pressure cup you have to understand the advantages and disadvantages of regulating the cup pressure. It's not impossible to learn, but it takes time.

Why do you think there's a reluctance of people to use HVLP?

There are a couple of reasons, and they're very legitimate. Everybody was very keyed up about HVLP at the start. There were lots of brand name guns and lots of articles and good press. But some of those big name guns were just converted high-pressure guns and they really didn't work very well. The performance of some of those was just terrible. People bought a lot of those and they were disappointed. So they blamed the technology; they figured HVLP was a bad idea. And so many people got into turbine systems early on, and some of those wouldn't keep up with the pace of a commercial shop.

You don't think turbine-powered systems are the answer for HVLP?

They aren't practical. If you look at where we're going with modern paints, solvents are something you will see a lot less of. Some of those solvents will be replaced with water. You are going to see thicker paint and paint with higher solids content. So the thicker the material, the harder it is for any paint equipment, high-pressure or HVLP, to break it up, to atomize that paint. If I were going to stay with lacquer paints, then a turbine might work fine.

Also, the turbine adds cost to the system. And of course you need to get the turbine out of the spray environment so then the hoses get long and that just makes the problem worse.

Some people say the CFM requirements of compressor-run HVLP guns are very high. What are the requirements of your compressor-driven guns? Will they work in hobby situations where

the painter doesn't always have enough compressor capacity?

The air cap that we developed last year, we call it the Air-Miser, it brings the gun down to where it will run off 9-12cfm (or 3-5hp). I can run a smaller horsepower compressor and not be waiting for the compressor to catch up. Three horsepower will work, but really you should still have 5hp. I use the conversion figure of 4cfm per horsepower. A big storage tank or lots of piping will help too.

Street rods are really a series of components, so it's easier to get by with a smaller compressor than the person who's painting a big van or a big sedan, for example.

The two traditional complaints are that HVLP is slow and that the guns are air hogs. Well, they are if they aren't set up right. Our equipment puts out a lot of material. If you were putting on three coats of clear, with our equipment you can achieve the same mill thickness with two coats.

In basecoat applications we get hiding a little faster. It lays the paint down uniformly. The reason your metallics float or sink, for example, depends on the velocity with which they hit the surface. A lot of velocity drives them right down to the bottom of the paint film. What I call sheer-impact leveling is beneficial for things like clearcoats. The sheer impact of the drops hitting the object tends to flatten out the paint film. With HVLP there is no sheer impact leveling. You have to have the solvent mix on the slower side of the solvent choice. You want to spray basecoats at typical gun-to-object distances like 8-10in or even 11in. But when you get to clearcoats and solid coverage objects, then you need to shoot at 6-8in.

Let's talk a little about solvent choice in various situations and how it's affected by HVLP equipment.

Well, the solvents we use to thin paints are rated as fast, medium, or slow, and this corresponds to the temperature recommendations you find on the cans of thinner or reducer. In general, a fast solvent is meant to be used in cool conditions like 55-65deg. Painters sometimes use a fast solvent on a hot day in order to get the paint to dry more quickly. What often happens, however, is the paint will flash quickly, but is really very slow to cure.

The kind of booth, or lack of a booth, also affects solvent choice. Paint manufacturers usually recommend that individuals working in open shop conditions use a somewhat faster solvent to compensate for the lack of air movement and the fact that dust control is always a problem.

With HVLP equipment, the painter should stay within the recommended temperature range (including considerations for shop conditions) but stay to the slower, or warmer, side of that range.

Do all HVLP guns put pressure on the paint in the pot?

Historically, yes. But recently some of the major manufacturers have taken the pressure off the pot as a means of simplifying the gun. These are siphon-style HVLP guns. People want to know if HVLP guns work better with pressure on the pot. Well, when you put pressure on the pot of a high-pressure gun the performance improves (many brand name high-pressure guns can be run off large pressurized containers of paint). Also, the transfer efficiency is higher with pressure on the pot. I think there are a lot of drawbacks to taking the pressure off the pot.

With our guns, you have the ability to regulate the pressure on the pot. This means you can compensate for materials with higher or lower solids content. If you don't have an adjustable pressure regulator on the pot, the only way to increase the amount of material coming out of the tip is with a larger fluid tip opening. The bigger hole means that bigger droplets of paint leave the gun, making it harder to correctly atomize the paint. By regulating the pressure on the pot you can increase the amount of material leaving the gun and still work with a small hole, thus assuring good atomization.

You increase the pressure to the point that you can force the paint through a small fluid tip, a smaller fluid tip gives you a smaller droplet, the pressure gives you the ounces of paint per minute—now I've got a happy medium of speed and a small droplet for good atomization, which leads to a smoother, flatter paint layout.

Look at a typical gun set-up for primer. It might have a fluid tip with a .090in hole; that's a pretty big hole. I can apply the same primer faster and get more of it to stay on the car—or get a thicker film built quicker—and the size of my fluid tip is less than .043in. So the pressurized pot is giving me a big advantage, and that is the ability to deliver a lot of paint without having to use a big hole. Thus, again, I've got the advantage of smaller droplets and great atomization.

Anyone who says an HVLP gun won't spray metallics, well, that individual has been exposed to the primer syndrome. Some people think HVLP is only good for primer, that it won't lay out a good flat finish paint. I can take a single-stage metallic—a hard thing to paint because you have to spray it wet enough for good gloss, and yet the metallics need good orientation—and do a good job of applying that paint with one of our HVLP guns.

Again, with metallics, we are able to use a relatively small hole in the fluid tip. I use a low cup pressure, like 3-4lb. And then I use 4-5lb at the air cap. The technique is to maintain your gun distance. Remember, you don't have the sheer impact to flatten the paint. You are basically just laying the metallics there, and they will stay there. You aren't driving them down into the bottom of the paint. Guys who have trouble spraying

Ross Mattson poses with one of the HVLP guns, developed by his late father Roy. Ross has worn many hats over the years, including custom painter, director of training (for PPG and Mattson), and co-developer of a custom painting system that was later sold to PPG to become the Radiance II product line.

metallics with HVLP probably have the gun set up to where it would be great for applying primer. They are over-wetting the paint, putting on too much material, and the metallics are sinking. HVLP isn't that much different than a high-pressure situation. People shouldn't get intimidated.

There are some good HVLP guns on the market. How does a person buy a good one that atomizes well and does a good job of applying the paint?

I guess you have to do some research, just like you might before buying a new stereo. You can't read *Consumer Reports*, but you can ask at some shops, find out what they're using. Ask people in the business. They use the equipment. The ads, of course, are often misleading. What you want is a good piece of equipment that will do a good job of applying the paint. If it doesn't lay down a nice coat of paint, it just isn't worth buying.

continued on next page

Where do first-time HVLP users get in trouble?

If I had my way, no one would be allowed to pick up one of our guns without looking at the training video first. Too often they pick up the gun, put on a fitting, and start spraying. They tell me that, "I've been in the business for twenty-five years, sonny. You aren't going to tell me anything about spraying paint." I hear that all the time, and if they would just learn a little about the gun first, they would have much better results. A lot of times they've got the gun set up all wrong with too high or too low a pot pressure and the wrong air cap pressure, too.

"Cheater" valves are a big no-no on HVLP equipment; you can't restrict the air flow. It is a correctly named device: It cheats the air supply to the gun, and you can't do that with HVLP. Quarter-inch hose is another problem. The hose must be at least 5/16, and 3/8in is the best.

Jobbers don't always take any time with the guy who buys that new gun, and the new owner goes out the door with the wrong fluid tip for the type of painting he's doing. Everybody knows what's the right fluid tip setup for a Binks number seven, but they don't all know what to do with a new HVLP gun, so the gun sometimes isn't set up correctly at the very beginning.

Some guys actually read the manual, take a little time to understand the equipment, and they usually turn into very happy customers.

In ten words or less, what advice have you got for first-time painters?

Fully access the information that each paint manufacturer puts out. If they don't put out good information, then don't use the product. If, as a manufacturer, I don't put out good information and training materials, then I haven't done my job. Look for and use the manuals, clinics, and seminars. We have to be painters, but painters willing to be educated. People in this business seem to want to hide or steam-roll their way through it. But it's all changing so fast, and there are more laws and regulations than ever before. But there's good news, too. You can now paint at a production level. You can save money on your paint job. You can now actually do a better paint job. The HVLP equipment has come a long way in just the last two years. Paint companies are starting to mix and blend their products to be easy to use with HVLP equipment. The paint is more user-friendly.

If you boil it all down, what is the difference between good and not-so-good spray painting equipment?

The key to any equipment is its ability to atomize properly. When we put on a two-day school we talk about how to get the equipment to properly atomize. That's the basic difference in our equipment—our stuff was designed by a painter to meet a painter's needs.

What I tell the beginning painters is to take advantage of the schools. Most major paint manufacturers, including both PPG and House of Kolor, put on schools and clinics. Mattson puts on its own school as well. There's no reason to make all the same mistakes I made when I was starting out. Take advantage of my experience or someone else's—learn to paint the right way the first time.

Chapter 3

Understanding Modern Paints

In the "good old days," choosing the paint was a pretty simple matter. There were enamels and nitrocellulose lacquers in a rather limited range of colors. Today, however, there are at least three types of finish paints in a bewildering array of colors, not to mention special finishes like metallics, pearls, and candy colors. Making sense of all this is easier if we first break the paint down to its basic components. Once you understand what's inside the paint can, it's easier to understand the three basic families of paints and the different types of primer materials.

What's Inside the Paint Can

Paint, any paint, is made up of three basic components: pigment, resin, and solvent, as well as a few additives.

Pigment is the material that gives the paint its color. Older paints often used lead-based pigments while modern paints have converted to nonlead pigments. One of the challenges for modern paint chemists is finding these new nontoxic pigments to take the place of the older lead-based materials.

Resin (also known as binder) helps to hold the pigments together and keep them sticking to the metal.

Solvent is the carrier used to make the paint thin enough to spray. In the case of lacquers, a true thinner is used, while in the case of an enamel the solvent is a reducer.

Additives are the materials added to the paint to give it a certain property or help it overcome a problem, much the way that additives are incorporated into modern oils to improve their performance.

If we're going to talk about paint, then there are a few more terms to cover. One that crops up more and more these days is VOCs, or volatile organic compounds. Another related term is solids, as in, "high-solids" paint.

Going back to the three basic components of paint, the solvent (a volatile material) evaporates (or oxidizes) after the paint is sprayed on the car, leaving behind the pigment and binder, known as the solids. Solvents that evaporate into the atmosphere are known in the industry as VOCs and they have come under government scrutiny in areas such as Southern California and New York City. These VOCs react with sunlight and can be a major contributor to smog.

Paint manufacturers are trying to increase the percentage of solids in their paints in order to reduce the amount of solvent, and thus reduce the VOC emissions. In the case of sandable primers, the high-solids term means that the primer contains a high percentage of solids and that these solids will fill scratches and small imperfections in the surface. (See the primer section farther along in this chapter for more on this.)

The Three Major Types of Paint

Most of the paints available for painting your hot rod can be classified as either a lacquer, an enamel, or a urethane. Though urethanes are technically an enamel, they will be considered here as a separate type of paint.

Enamel

Enamels have been used to cover everything from Fords to Frigidaires. Most modern enamels are acrylic enamels (meaning they contain plastic), offering better flexibility and durability than the older alkyd enamel. Many modern enamel paints can be catalyzed with isocyanate, which aids cross-linking of the paint molecules, thus improving the durability of the finish.

Enamel uses a reducer instead of a thinner as the solvent part of the mix. An enamel paint job hardens as the reducer evaporates *and* the resin oxidizes (as it mixes with oxygen). You might not give a darn about evaporation or oxidation until you realize that the need for oxidation adds considerably to the drying time of an enamel paint job.

Acrylic enamel makes a fine finish though most custom painters shy away from the material because the long drying time means more time for dust to be trapped on the surface of the paint, and more time to wait to apply second coats or tape out a design. You will find, too, that most of what we call "custom" paints are available as either a urethane or an acrylic lacquer.

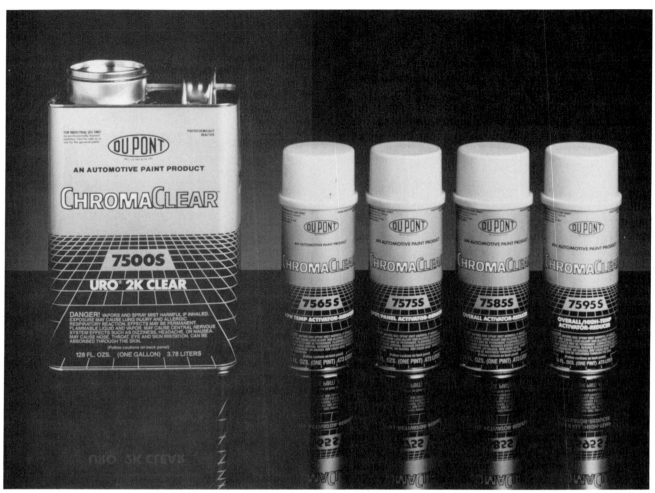

ChromaClear is a catalyzed urethane clear from DuPont designed to clearcoat ChromaBase and other basecoats. The different activator/reducers are designed to cover different temperatures and shop conditions.

Lacquer

Lacquer paints have been available for years and years. During the early fifties, most of the custom cars and bikes were painted with lacquer, nitrocellulose lacquer to be exact. This early lacquer was easy to work with and offered some vibrant colors, but there were at least two major drawbacks. First, nitrocellulose is a toxic material, and second, those early lacquer paint jobs tended to crack with age due to the paint's inability to flex. By the late fifties everyone had switched to a new lacquer formula—acrylic lacquer. This new material eliminated the toxic nitrocellulose, while the addition of the acrylic provided better resistance to ultraviolet radiation and also gave the paint more flexibility. The increased flexibility helped to eliminate most of the cracking that occurred with the earlier material.

Custom painters have always liked lacquer because of its fast drying times, low toxicity (for the acrylic lacquers), great color, and the ease with which spot repairs can be made. Custom painters often put lacquer on in multiple coats, wet sanding between coats. The end result is a deep shine that you can almost swim in and a perfectly smooth surface created by all the sanding between coats.

The trouble with acrylic lacquer is its lack of durability (it chips and stains fairly easily) and the large amount of maintenance a lacquer paint job requires. The great lacquer shine comes only after plenty of wet sanding and polishing. Keeping the paint looking good usually means regular sessions with polish and wax. In the end, a good looking lacquer paint job requires a lot of work.

The other problem with lacquer paints is the VOC issue discussed earlier. The evaporating thinner and the multiple coats (more thinner) mean that spraying lacquer puts a relatively large amount of VOCs in the atmosphere. People within the industry predict that the day will come when lacquer will no longer be available, though no one seems to know exactly when that will be.

Urethane

The hot stuff in the custom painting field is urethane. What's urethane? Technically, urethane is an enamel, yet it sprays much like a lacquer. Urethane is a relatively new two-part paint material catalyzed with isocyanate. Even though it's classified as an enamel, urethane dries very fast and offers easy spot repairs. The fast drying means quick application of second coats, easy candy paint jobs, and fast tape-outs for flame jobs and graphics. Unlike lacquer, urethane is extremely durable, resisting rock chips and chemical stains better than anything except powder coating.

Urethane can be used in a basecoat-clearcoat situation or as a single-stage application. Because of their durability, urethanes are a good choice for frames, suspension components, and engine cases.

The biggest single downside to the urethane paints is the toxicity of the catalyst, the isocyanate. These materials are so toxic that spraying with urethanes requires a fresh-air system (especially in the home shop painting situation, where ventilation is limited) so the painter is sure to breathe absolutely *no* shop air. The other downside to urethanes is their higher cost.

Custom Paints

Custom paint jobs are often applied in multiple layers. The first finish coat is called the basecoat. This base layer of paint can be any color or a metallic paint. The basecoat can be covered by a candycoat, a clearcoat, or both.

Candy colors were discovered in the fifties when custom painters like Jon Kosmoski tried putting a little tint in a can of clear and then sprayed the tinted clear over the base color. The final color in a candy paint job is a combination of the base color as seen through the tinted coat on top. The effect is much like looking through a piece of translucent colored candy, thus the name. These new candy paint jobs became the hot ticket for custom cars and remain so to this day. By combining different basecoats with different candy colors (and a different number of candycoats) an infinite number of colors are possible.

Sometimes the basecoat is simply covered with a clearcoat on top. Clearcoats have become common on new cars and provide good protection from both ultraviolet rays and harsh chemicals, and provide a great shine, too. Some of the basecoats dry with a flat finish because the shine is provided by the clearcoat.

Most modern candy paint jobs contain three distinct layers of paint. The basecoat (often a metallic or semimetallic color), followed by the candycoat, and then topped by a clearcoat for a great shine and good protection for the paint job.

Most of us are familiar with metallic paint, when tiny pieces of "tin foil" are added to the paint by the manufacturer or the painter to provide extra sparkle. Metallics are currently available from a number of suppliers in different sizes and various colors (though silver and gold remain the most popular).

Metallics add sparkle to a paint job; pearls, on the other hand, add a more subtle glow in much the same way. Pearl particles are tiny bits of synthetic material added to the paint. The glow of a pearl job comes from the light that strikes the pearl flake and is then reflected to the viewer. The actual color you see depends on the color of the pearl particles, often acting in combination with the color of the basecoat or the tinted clearcoat.

Pearl paint jobs often react differently to different types and angles of light. Walking around a pearl job can be a little unsettling. From one direction you might see the blue basecoat, while from another you see the violet color reflected by the colored pearl chips. A good pearl job has a lovely soft glow almost as though the light is shining through the paint from underneath—thus the name.

Primer Materials

The finest candy paint job in the world won't last long if the preparation and materials used under the finish paint aren't of the highest quality. First-time painters often think primer is just primer. Wrong. Primer comes in

EP-2 (and Kwikure KP-2) are two-part primer-surfacers from House of Kolor. Unlike some primer-surfacers, this product can also be used as a pure primer, or the very first coat of paint applied to bare metal.

"Metal flakes" are available from a variety of manufacturers. These Flakes from House of Kolor come in three sizes and a number of colors. Jon recommends that the flakes be added directly to the clearcoat sprayed over the basecoat. The color and amount of flake you use depends on the color of the basecoat and personal preference.

lacquer and two-part (often known as epoxy primer), as a sealer and as a primer-surfacer.

Wax and Grease Removers

Wax and grease remover isn't even a paint, yet it is the first thing you should use on the surface before applying any kind of paint. If it ain't clean, the paint won't stick—period.

Metal Prep

If you've stripped the body and fenders to their birthday suits, then you probably need to use a metal etch before spraying the first coat of primer. The metal etch prepares the bare metal for the primer. Though many shops spray epoxy primer over bare steel, many paint manufacturers recommend you treat the steel with metal etch first. Think of it as a primer for the primer.

Primer

A true primer is a paint material chosen for its good adhesion to the material it is sprayed over. Most provide good resistance to corrosion and moisture. A true primer is not meant to be sanded and contains a low percent-

age of solids.

There is a lot of talk lately about the new water-based primers. These new primers have been introduced to minimize VOCs and toxic materials, and they actually replace only some of the solvents found in a standard primer with water.

Primer-Surfacer

Primer-surfacers are primer materials with a high-solids content. While offering good adhesion like a straight primer, a primer-surfacer will help fill small scratches and imperfections, and sands easily. Primer-surfacers should be applied in two or three thin coats and then sanded when dry. If you fail to allow the material to dry properly before sanding, it will shrink *after* you've finished sanding, allowing small scratches (known as sand scratches) to show through the finished paint job.

Epoxy Primer

An epoxy (or two-part) primer like DP 40 from PPG or EP-2 from House of Kolor is a more durable, expensive, primer material. These materials are known for their superior bonding abilities and great corrosion resistance. The catalyst in these paints (at least in the case of PPG and House of Kolor products) is not an isocyanate. Most painters spray these materials with only a charcoal-type respirator. It should be noted that PPG recommends a fresh-air hood in spite of the fact that there are no isocyanates in these products.

Some of these, such as the EP-2 and KP-2 from House of Kolor, can be sanded like a primer-surfacer, while others are meant to be used as a strict primer. Many of these can be used as the sealer coat before the color coats are applied. Though they are durable and useful materials, each is a little different so be sure to check the manufacturer's recommendations.

Primer-Sealer

A primer-sealer, sometimes known as a sealer, is meant to seal or separate two different layers of paint. A coat of sealer is often applied as the final coat of "primer" before starting with the first of the finish coats. This is not a sandable finish, but is meant to seal two different types of paint. For example, lacquer sprayed over enamel will often cause a reaction between the two paints, so a sealer is applied before the lacquer is applied. (Enamel sprayed over lacquer isn't usually a problem, though a sealer should be used anyway.)

The other advantage of using a primer-sealer is to achieve good color hold-out. Sometimes the final coat(s) of paint will soak into the primer coats underneath. This dulls and changes the color of the final coat. Color hold-out means the top or final coats are "held out" and prevented from mixing in any way with the paint underneath. This means the Porsche Guards Red you spray on will look like and remain looking like the color chip in the paint book.

Adhesion Promoter

Adhesion promoters are similar in intent to primer-sealers and are sometimes used to ensure that one coat of paint will stick to the older paint underneath.

Paint Compatibility

As stated earlier, it's dangerous to spray lacquer over enamel, less so to spray enamel over lacquer. You may wonder whether the paint on your hot rod is lacquer or not. Well, just take a little lacquer thinner to a hidden spot and see if it dissolves the paint. Before spraying over an old paint job, remember that it isn't just a matter of which type of paints work with another type. You can only put the paint on so thick before it starts to crack, no matter what type of paint it is. If the old paint looks thick and shows any cracks, then it's probably already too thick. Jon Kosmoski feels that the modern lacquer jobs that crack do so simply because the paint is too thick.

So, when in doubt about whether or not to put more layers over an old paint job, there's one simple answer: Don't. By stripping the paint you eliminate all the hassles of compatibility and too many layers of paint. By working from bare metal you control all the steps in the painting process and are thus better able to ensure success. You will discover and eliminate any old bodywork and start over fresh. By discovering and repairing any old repairs you eliminate one more thing that might ruin your new paint job (see chapter 4 for more on paint stripping).

Polish

Though polish isn't a paint at all, anyone who intends to paint will need to know something about polish. Despite our best efforts, many paint jobs come out of the garage with small imperfections in the top layer of paint or the final clearcoat.

As a general rule, you should never sand or rub a candy color or a pearl. These paints are clearcoated, so any sanding or polishing you do is done to the clearcoat. A number of paint care companies have products or an entire system of products intended for polishing paint. Well known for their car care products, the Meguiar's company's paint care products are available in many auto and motorcycle shops. The number of products in either their professional or amateur lines is mind-boggling.

One question that crops up during any discussion of polishing is the use of a power buffer—whether to use one, and if so, how to use one. A representative from Meguiar's reports, "Most of our products work better with a power buffer, but when a person—especially an amateur—is in doubt about whether or not to use power, the answer is to do it by hand." Meguiar's does make a set of special buffing tools and accessories for use with their specific products.

The company recommends that you start the polishing with wet, 2,000 grit sandpaper (if the imperfections are minor, you could skip the sandpaper and start with the liquid polish). The next step is their number two liq-

uid cleaner from their professional line, followed by their number nine fine-cut polish, followed by a good carnauba wax. Remember, it's easy to rub through, especially at any kind of edge, even when you're working by hand. Use a cotton towel (no wool pads or towels) large enough to fit the palm of your hand, and be careful to stay away from any edges or raised areas. Remember, too, that urethane clear is a much tougher film than lacquer, and rub accordingly.

Some painters start the polishing with 600 grit wet to really flatten the paint (be sure you've got a thick enough film of paint before starting in like this), then move to 1,200 and finally 2,000, before going on to the polishing system of their choice. 3M makes a variety of products designed to be used in sequence. The 3M system includes both compounds and buffing pads; note the materials used for buffing in both chapters 5 and 6.

Most painters finish the polishing sequence with a good glaze product applied by hand to eliminate any swirl marks, fill tiny cracks in the paint, and really bring out the paint's shine.

What All This Means

The new paints are better than ever, more durable, and colorful than anything seen before. There are, of course, a few things you have to keep in mind.

These easy-to-apply pearls are from House of Kolor and can simply be clearcoated or used as a base for candy colors. When using pearls, Jon recommends that the painter be careful with preparation and the type of filler used because pearls are prone to stains and bleeding from the filler.

Meguiar's makes a wide variety of paint care products. The number nine is classified as a cleaner-polish and is often used in combination with 2,000 grit sandpaper and their number two fine-cut cleaner to rub out fresh clearcoats. Also very popular with hot rodders is the number seven, Show Car glaze, designed to "outshine all other hand applied polishes, glazes, or waxes."

Each manufacturer makes an information sheet available for each product. These sheets contain a wealth of information regarding the mixing, use, and application of the paint. Should you follow one light coat with a heavy coat? How long are the flash times? How long before you can apply or remove tape? All these questions and more are answered in the product information sheets.

Strangely, safety information is *not* included in most of these information sheets, so you must rely on the labels on the cans or ask for the safety data sheets for each product.

Speaking of safety, be sure to use a charcoal-type respirator in *any* painting situation, except where isocyanates are involved, in which case you need a separate fresh-air system. You can find more on safety in chapter 2.

Most modern paints have evolved into "systems" designed by each manufacturer to answer a certain need. Once you've decided which type of paint job you're going to apply, then try to stick with one type of paint from one manufacturer. If you're spraying acrylic lacquer, use lacquer for the base, candy, and clearcoat. Try to buy all the paint from one manufacturer—probably as part of that manufacturer's system. By using basecoat, candycoat, and clearcoat from one manufacturer, you know all the paints are designed to work together and will be totally compatible.

If you have any questions about compatibility be sure to ask the paint supplier. There's nothing worse than slaving over a great paint job only to have the paint wrinkle when you spray on the clearcoat. Though primers and sealers are pretty universal, never use one company's catalyst with another company's urethane paint.

Professional painters sometimes cheat and put a particular urethane clear over an acrylic lacquer candy job. It may work fine for them, but it's just not a good idea for the rest of us.

Both House of Kolor and PPG make basecoats that contain no isocyanates and can be cleared with either urethane or lacquer. By clearing these paints with lacquer, (as long as we can still buy lacquer) you can do a paint job at home that's free of any isocyanates and requires no renting or buying of a fresh-air system.

In order to do a successful paint job, you need to remember a few key rules of the painted road:
· Be careful with the preparation
· Use one type of paint from one manufacturer whenever possible
· Keep the temperature in the shop at least 70deg
· And read the directions.

This Thom Taylor rendering makes good use of flames. Note that the flames start in an orange-red and fade to white, the reverse of most flamed color patterns.

Built several years ago, the Vern Luce Coupe looks contemporary today—due to its timeless good looks built on a good design and good use of color.

This is the Model A coupe built by Jeff Stanke at the Twin
Town shop. Note the traditional touches like the headlight
bar, door hinges, and stainless grille shell.

This rear view of the Model A coupe built by Jeff Stanke
shows off the flawless body work and great paint. The results
of the careful prep work and endless block sanding don't show
up until the job is all done—and it's too late to go back and
re-do any of the work hidden under the paint.

Hot rods don't have to be white, in spite of tradition. White works for some cars and lends them a very sanitary look.

Some people would argue for the addition of pinstripes or graphics on this white Deuce. Whether the additional color would make it better or worse is ultimately a matter of taste.

When a car is choice enough, it looks outstanding even in plain black primer, like this car that Boyd built for Jamie Musselman. Its fiberglass body rides on a Boyd-built chassis, and the paint, while basic, still looks stunning.

This is the very red, very smooth Ford coupe painted at the Unique Shop by Ron Gorrel.

This pair of red aces (Deuces, actually) belong to Bruce Corzine. They were painted by Greg Morrell in Boyd's shop. The pinstriping that runs the length of the convertible is a fine example of subtlety; two clean stripes provide adequate accent and the clean look of these cars would be spoiled by overly ornate striping.

A yellow 1933 Ford C-400 convertible (a car that never really existed—until created in Boyd's shop) has a Beige top and no pinstripes—tasteful and understated to the max.

This Ford coupe carries the classic paint job, yellow flames over a hot-rod red paint job.

This close-up shows the Dennis Ricklef flame pattern, a yellow with blended areas of light red, all pinstriped in a lime green.

Another Dennis Ricklef flame job, this time on a massaged Deuce built by the boys at Boyd's.

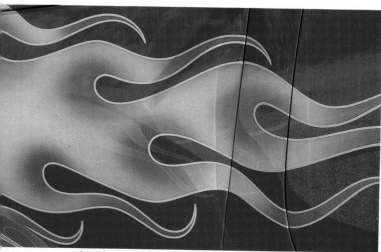

This close-up of the flames painted by Dennis Ricklef shows the blended areas and the neat, thin pinstriping.

Below
The legendary CadZZilla is the type of car most of us can only dream of. Its eggplant purple paint (laid over a gray base) is a fine example of how a candy paint job has a chameleon-like ability to seemingly change color. When you see it from one view, CadZZilla looks almost black. From another angle, or in slightly different light, it has a deep ruby purple cast.

This might be part of the reason why most home-built rods don't quite look like Boyd-built machines. The paint on this chassis and engine from Boyd's is meticulous. While you might not see much of the painted frame once your car is completed, your engine and engine bay will frequently be on display, so a well-done paint job there can add greatly to the car's appeal.

Chapter 4

Bodywork and Preparation

Most of the material in this chapter on preparation is taken from the *Boyd Coddington's How To Build Hot Rod Bodywork* book. This is not intended as a complete bodywork section but is included here for the individual who needs a little refresher on the work that should be done before the paint is applied. And because you might need to remove paint before applying a fresh paint job, I have included the paint stripping information, also from that earlier book.

Working with Body Filler: Body Fillers and Spot Putties

Once a dent has been worked as smooth as possible with hammer and dolly, you're left with the task of filling it with some kind of body filler. Everyone knows about plastic filler (often known as bondo), or at least they think they do. In reality, there are at least three distinct types of plastic body filler.

Basic body filler is usually a polyester plastic combined with a cream hardener. Sold by numerous companies under a variety of trade names, this basic bondo is very useful and can be used over most metals and in most situations requiring body filler.

A second type, lightweight body filler, is offered by many companies and contains tiny pieces of polystyrene. The small particles make the lightweight fillers easier to sand and work. Some customizers like to use this material to mold the frames, as the easy sanding properties are much appreciated where there's a great deal of intricate hand sanding.

The third type of bondo is known as "stain-free." Jim McGill from PPG explained what the stain-free label means: "Sometimes when you apply a light color or a light pearl paint over filler, especially if you used too much hardener in the filler, a stain develops under the paint that can be seen through the paint. What actually happens is a reaction between the paint and the peroxides in the hardener used with the body filler. The sunlight sets off the reaction or acts as kind of a catalyst, but once the stain is there it never goes away.

"Anytime you intend to use a light pastel or pearl paint, use stain-free filler. The only other way to avoid the

Body filler comes in at least three variations: The lightweight filler shown here, regular filler, and stain free body filler meant for certain light colored paint jobs.

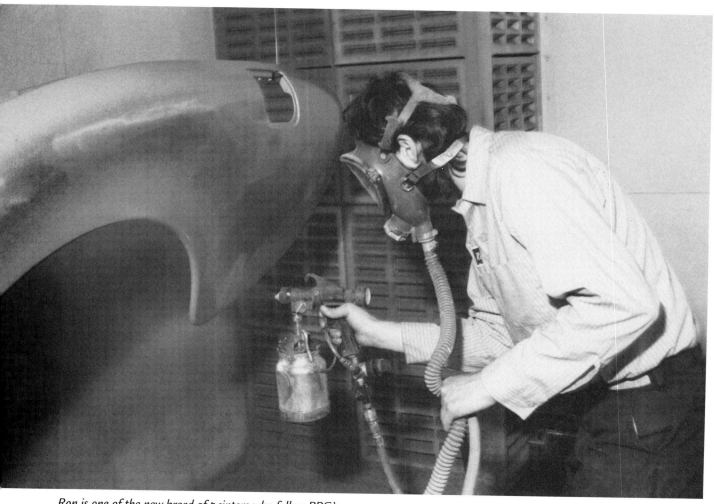

Ron is one of the new breed of painters who follow PPG's recommendation that filler be applied over a good two-part primer rather than over bare steel. Here Ron sprays the fender with DP 50 from PPG.

stain is to apply two coats of black (not primer black) before applying the final paint to act as an absorber coat. The black absorbs any peroxides and acts as an absorber between the paint and the filler. A regular sealer or primer-sealer isn't good enough to prevent the reaction."

Do's and Don'ts of Bondo Use

Since the days when body men (they were all men in those days) put aside their paddles and files for working lead and took up the plastic filler instead, filler has been successfully applied over bare steel. Now, thirty-some years after the conversion from lead to plastic, at least one manufacturer is recommending that the plastic filler be spread over properly prepared steel that has been painted with its two-part primer.

First, we need to back up and talk about what constitutes a properly prepared piece of steel. Body filler bonds to the steel in two ways: mechanically and chemi-

cally. The mechanical link requires some roughness to the surface so the bondo can "grip" the metal. Most manufacturers and most of the people applying filler day in and day out recommend that the steel be cleaned bare and then sanded with a 36 grit grinding pad. The deep scratches left from the 36 grit pad aid the mechanical part of the bond between filler and steel.

Everyone agreed that, until recently, the chemical part of the bond worked best when the filler was applied over bare steel. Now PPG, a major paint and filler manufacturer, recommends otherwise. Jim McGill explains that you still need to grind the metal with a 36 grit pad to provide the mechanical part of the bond, but that "you actually get a better chemical bond between bondo and our two-part primer (like DP 40) than between bondo and bare steel."

Jon Kosmoski, owner of House of Kolor, a painter and paint manufacturer for over thirty years, feels other-

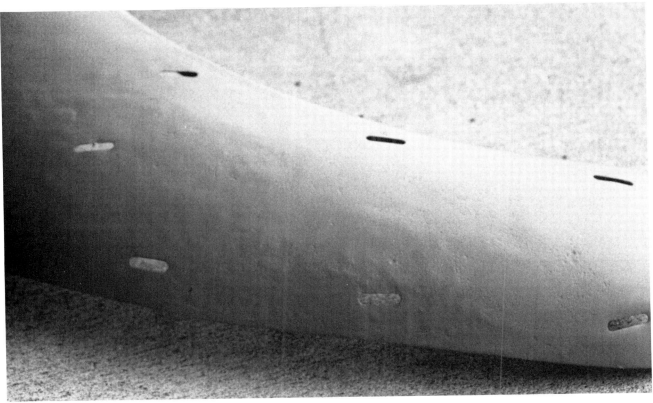

Here we see the front of the fender before the first coat of filler is applied. Filler should go on within the window of time specified by the manufacturer to create a good bond with the paint.

wise: "We always put the bondo on over bare steel, never over a primer—not PPG's two-part or our own EP-2 and KP-2 primer."

A survey taken in the "real world" of small bodyshops and customizing operations indicates that most filler is still being applied over bare steel, in spite of what PPG recommends.

Back to the list of do's and don'ts: Always make sure the temperature is at least 60deg in your shop, and preferably higher. Otherwise you get condensation between the cool steel and the hot bondo (the chemical reaction that occurs as the filler hardens creates heat). Condensation can weaken the chemical bond and start the metal rusting—further weakening the bond.

Always mix the filler and hardener according to the instructions. Attempts to speed up the hardening by adding extra hardener can cause the finished bondo to be brittle or soft.

Gordy Larson, known to friends as "The Bondo Wizard," adds a few hints: "You have to mix the bondo and hardener thoroughly and then apply it to the steel with firm pressure to minimize air bubbles. Air bubbles are most common when it's hot out. The bubbles seem to form as the bondo cures. The air bubbles cause little pinholes that show up after the bondo is sanded. I fill

The important things about mixing filler are that you knead the hardener first, use the filler and hardener in the correct ratios per the instructions, and that the two materials be thoroughly mixed before application.

43

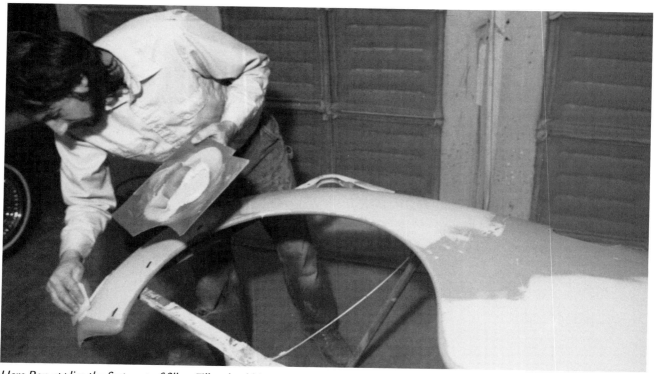

Here Ron applies the first coat of filler. Filler should be put on with a firm hand to minimize air bubbles and increase adhe- sion. Ron mixes only as much filler as he can put on in a short period of time, so he's not fighting it as it begins to set up.

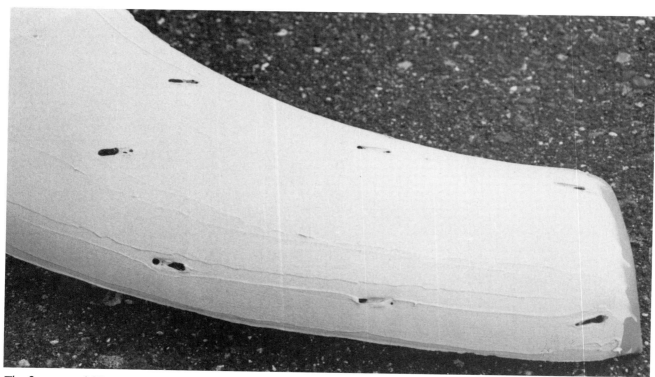

The first coat of filler is intended to fill the worst of the low spots and give the fender shape. This close up shows the front of the fender after the first application of filler. The material is about 1/16in thick. Ron will clean out the mounting holes for the rock guard a little later.

these with just a little more bondo pushed into the holes with a single-edge razor blade. Spot putty would work too.

"I always put on at least two coats of bondo. The first coat I sand with 36 grit after it has set up. Then I put on a thinner second coat and sand that with 80 grit. Then the next step is usually primer-surfacer, unless there are pinholes in the second coat of bondo. Primer won't fill pinholes so you have to fill those with more bondo or spot putty."

Spot putties come in various types and brands. Think of these as somewhere between primer-surfacer and body filler in terms of solids content and applications. Most can be applied to imperfections too small to require the mixing of a batch of bondo. Most of these putties dry fast and sand easily. While body filler should go on over bare steel or more filler (or two-part primer in some cases), spot putties can be applied over paint. You can fill low spots that show up after the first coat of primer has been applied without sanding back down to the bare steel. Any spot putty you use should be a two-part catalyzed product.

Hands On: A Buick Fender Gets Smooth and Ready for Paint

The book *Boyd Coddington's How To Build Hot Rod Bodywork* included a demonstration project on a Buick fender with help from Ron Gorrell at Unique Body and Paint in Blaine, Minnesota. What follows is the body filler part of that project.

After working the dents out as much as possible with hammer and dolly, Ron prepares to apply the first coat of filler. Ron prefers to put his filler on over an epoxy primer, but before the first coat of primer can be applied there is just one more thing. A few little rusty areas were left over from the stripping process, and those are cleaned with a small sandblaster. The fender is then cleaned with wax and grease remover, then sprayed with epoxy primer.

Because the fender sat for two days before we could get back to the project, Ron starts the next step by scuffing the paint with a Scotch-Brite pad to ensure that the filler will stick. It's another case of following the directions on the can—most primer products are designed to have the next layer applied during a "window" of time.

These are the basic tools that Ron uses for shaping the filler. On the left is the mud hog, Ron's tool of choice for working the filler. He starts with a 36 grit pad and then moves to an 80 grit pad.

When you go past this window you need to scuff the surface or recoat the panel. After scuffing the panel Ron wipes it down with wax and grease remover.

Ron mixes the filler on a piece of sheet metal, being careful to mix in just the right amount of hardener, not too much or too little because it affects the strength and shrinkage of the finished filler. During the mixing Ron explains that: "I always knead the hardener in the tube, because it can separate in the tube, and I'm real careful to mix the hardener completely with the filler material."

The first coat of filler is spread evenly on the fender in a coat about 1/16in thick, across nearly the entire area of the fender. The only area that doesn't get coated is an undamaged section of metal near the gas-filler opening. By keeping the total area to be coated fairly small, Ron is able to limit the amount of filler he is mixing and applying. "I never mix more filler than I can apply pretty quick. Otherwise it's starting to set up as you apply it," says Ron. "And I push it on real hard when I apply it so I get good adhesion and minimize any air bubbles in the filler."

Ron waits until the next day to begin working the filler. The shaping and sanding starts with a 36 grit pad on a "mud hog," or large D-A with a foam pad. Ron keeps the speed of the disc rather low with the air-trigger and slowly shapes the panel. Though the mud hog tends to take off the high spots, and that's what you want, it's important that all the filler be sanded so the second coat of filler will adhere to the first.

The first coat of filler is typically used to fill and correct the worst of the highs and lows in the panel. Coat number two is considered a finish coat. Sometimes a

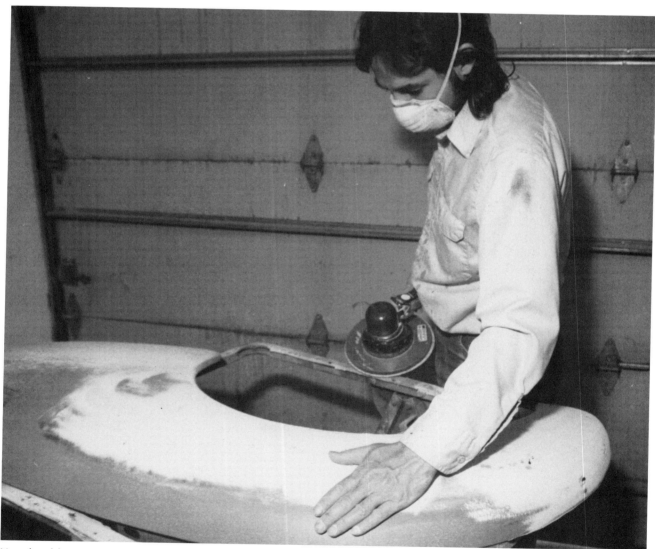

Your hand becomes a very important tool—here Ron checks the shape of the filler and the location of the high and low areas.

46

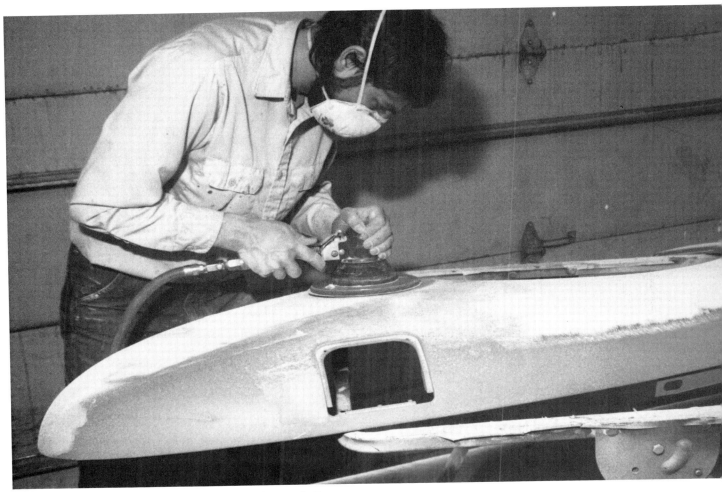

Shaping the first coat of filler is done by keeping the speed of the pad low and constantly moving it across the fender. Ron is careful to get down into the low spots with the 36 grit pad so that the second coat of filler will adhere to the first.

third coat of filler is needed in certain areas.

Before applying the second coat of filler, Ron cleans the fender and prepares it for more filler. First, he blows off all the loose filler dust. Next, the metal part of the fender (with no filler on it) is scuffed again with the Scotch-Brite pad. After cleaning the fender, Ron puts on another coat of epoxy primer to act as the base for the second coat of filler.

The second coat of filler is applied to the entire surface of the fender, in a thinner application than the first coat. After allowing the filler to set up, Ron starts the finish work with the mud hog again, equipped with a 36 grit pad. Ron quickly sands down the high spots and changes to an 80 grit pad. During this process of sanding, the speed of the disc is kept low, and Ron stops occasionally to check the progress of the finishing operation.

Once Ron has the fender shaped reasonably well, he puts away the power tools and starts working the flat surfaces with an idiot stick equipped with 80 grit sandpaper. Surfaces too rounded for the stick, such as the tail end of the fender, for example, are worked with a flexible sanding pad and 80 grit paper.

Ron explains that as the fender takes shape, you might want to apply a light coat of lacquer primer in a color that contrasts with the filler, to act as a "guide coat." A guide coat simply guides the sanding and finish work by making the low spots really obvious.

When he's happy with the shape of the fender, Ron cleans it again and then applies three coats of two-part primer-surfacer. This high-solids primer material is really a filler used to fill the sand scratches and any very slight low spots that might remain on the surface of the fender. The product Ron uses is Prima from PPG, though there are a number of similar products on the market.

Before starting the next stage of finishing, Ron applies a light coat of a contrasting lacquer primer. This paint is sprayed on to act as a guide coat. When Ron starts the next step in the sanding sequence, he uses a small, flexible pad and 120 grit paper. The guide coat comes off quickly, except in the low spots, which become very obvious.

As he works the surface of the fender, Ron uses a paint-stirring stick slapped against the paper on the sanding block to loosen the accumulations of paint. In this way he gets a lot more mileage from each piece of sandpaper.

Ron advises against sanding through the primer-surfacer down into the filler material: "You just make trouble for yourself, you open up little pinholes, and sometimes you undo a lot of good shaping work that was done earlier. It's better to just find the low spots, apply another two coats of primer-surfacer and sand the fender again. Usually the second application of primer-surfacer fills any little low spots you find while you're sanding with 120 the first time."

After sanding the entire fender with 120 on a flexible block, Ron applies two more coats of primer-surfacer, one light guide coat, and then the final wet sanding with 320 grit.

The important parts of this process are well documented. Ron followed a logical plan with well defined stages. Each stage or step has its place and shouldn't be skipped or substituted for another. As for final words of wisdom, Ron says: "People should learn to wait for the full dry-time recommended for each product—and they've got to be patient."

Tips for Painting that 'glass Body

Here, from a variety of expert sources, are some helpful hints for finishing and painting fiberglass.

Everyone agrees on the need to clean and scuff the gelcoat before applying the first coat of paint. At least one fiberglass manufacturer feels that "stars" on the fenders are often caused by primer that didn't adhere to the fiberglass—the impact of the rocks is enough to jar the paint loose from the fender if the paint wasn't really stuck to the 'glass.

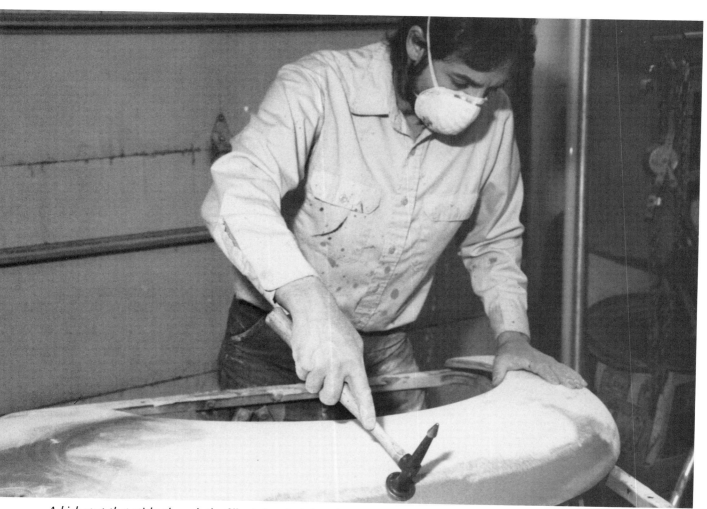

A high spot that sticks through the filler is knocked down before the next coat of filler is applied.

Some manufacturers use a mold release agent that contains silicones, so it's a good idea to start the pre-paint activities by cleaning the body with a cleaner such as Prep Sol. Next, you want to scuff the gelcoat with 320 grit (some would suggest 180 grit) sandpaper to ensure that the first coat of primer or filler can bite into the fiberglass. The first coat of primer should be a brand name, two-part primer, as these products bond with more tenacity to the 'glass body. Any fillers or putties used on the 'glass should be a two-part product as well. If you're using bondo, then you want to use a coarse grinding pad on the area where the bondo will be applied—just as you would with a metal body. Greg and Keith from Boyd's recommend that if you sand through the gelcoat, you apply more gelcoat to the body (with a polyester resin-type product like SEM Prime, or just gelcoat) before moving on to fillers or primer-surfacers.

The primer-surfacer you use to block out any imperfections in the body should probably be the product rec-ommended by the paint supply house, something that's sure to be compatible with the primer.

Painting fiberglass is often complicated by static electricity. The static electricity attracts dirt, yet seems to repel the paint. At Wescott's, where they build fiberglass bodies, they recommend starting with an ultra-clean shop and then grounding *everything*, including the gun, the car, and the painter (I'm not kidding).

Ross Mattson recommends wiping the vehicle down with isopropyl alcohol as a good means of eliminating static electricity, while Greg at Boyd's says that multiple passes with the tack rag seem to help combat the static problem.

For more on painting fiberglass, see the procedures used for painting the fiberglass fenders in chapter 5.

Paint Stripping

Most of us drag a lot of stuff home, and most of that junk leaves a lot to be desired. The treasures we bring into the garage are usually covered with old paint,

Ron applies the second coat of filler (this is usually the final coat though sometimes a third coat is needed) after cleaning off all the dust from the earlier sanding.

rust, crust, body filler, lead, and who knows what else. Before proceeding with repair or repaint, the parts need to be taken down to bare metal.

If the piece in question is rusty sheet metal, there isn't much you can do with it until you've eliminated the rust. There are other reasons besides rust for stripping all the old paint off any part. By getting down to bare metal you eliminate worries about reactions between the old paint and your new paint or problems created by too many layers of paint. You also discover (sometimes painfully) any old repairs in need of further repair.

The various stripping methods break down into four basic processes: blasting, dipping, chemical stripping, and sanding. Each has advantages and disadvantages. What follows is a look at each method and some hands-on examples of two of the more popular methods.

Blasting

The best known blasting technique is sandblasting, definitely an aggressive method of paint removal. Though this mechanical process may work well for large, heavy objects like frame rails and transmission cases, there are some problems when sandblasting is used on sheet metal. First, the stream of sand propelled by high-pressure air hits the sheet metal with tremendous force, and that force and abrasion creates heat, which often warps the sheet metal.

Second, the pits created by the sandblasting stretch the metal, causing more warpage. If that weren't enough, the heat causes embrittlement of the steel. Finally, the little bits of sand don't get down into the pores to eliminate all the rust. So while you may be able to use one of the little home sandblasters on small areas of sheet metal, don't ever let one of the commercial blasting operations go after that nice coupe body.

Plastic blasting has become popular on a commercial scale and evolved into a whole new industry. Less aggressive than sandblasting, this process can be used to remove paint without attacking and warping the metal itself. Plastic blasting methods were developed about 1979 as a safe means of stripping paint from military aircraft. The military wanted a method of removing paint that wouldn't damage the thin aluminum, and a method that didn't create an environmental disaster with a lot of toxic stripping chemicals. If the plastic particles won't warp the aluminum panels on a military airplane, you can bet it's safe to use on your Deuce roadster or '55 Chevy.

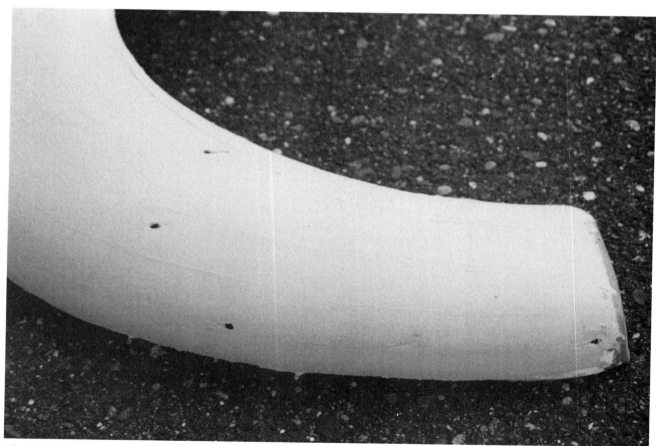

The close up shows the front of the fender following application of the second—and much thinner—coat of filler.

50

The particles themselves are made from thermoset plastic, and each particle has sharp edges designed to cut paint without the need for high air pressure. Dennis Norgaard, owner of Strip Rite in Fridley, Minnesota, showed me the little plastic particles. "We actually have a choice of two particles that we can use," explained Dennis. "Both are someplace between walnut shells and glass beads in terms of hardness. One is slightly smaller and softer, we use it on delicate surfaces like fiberglass Corvettes and some aluminum panels. The other particles are just a little bigger and harder, and we use those on most other surfaces."

The length of time it takes to strip a part or a body shell depends on its size, the type of paint being removed, and the number of paint layers. Dennis never gives an estimate. "I can usually ballpark the price, but the actual amount we charge is determined by a meter that runs whenever the gun is running. Once we start on a project, we can usually tell if it's going to be especially tough to do."

For comparison, I asked Dennis to strip the paint off a Model A front fender, one with a relatively thin layer of paint. Removing all the paint from the fender took about ten minutes. As you can see from the pictures, all the paint is gone, and any rust in the pits or on the back side is left intact.

In terms of actual dollar cost, a body shell that doesn't have sixteen coats of catalyzed urethane on it will run roughly $350 to $400. Dennis says that it never costs more than it would to chemically strip the body at a commercial bodyshop. Dennis and his wife, Sandy, schedule carefully and can often offer one-day turnaround. In addition to the blasting time, Dennis and crew have the added time of preparation—not a problem if it's a bare body shell—and cleanup when they're finished.

"One of the really nice things about our process is our ability to strip the entire car without forcing the customer to completely disassemble it," says Dennis. "A lot of people leave the glass in the car, the door handles on. It's up to the customer."

The plastic stripping process is so delicate that a good operator can actually take the paint off one layer at a time—leaving the factory primer intact if that's what the customer wants as much. Plastic body filler is left alone, unless the customer wants it all removed. The equipment runs on a high volume of relatively low-pressure air—20 to 40lb. Dennis says that though he can run up to 40lb, "I never use more than 30psi."

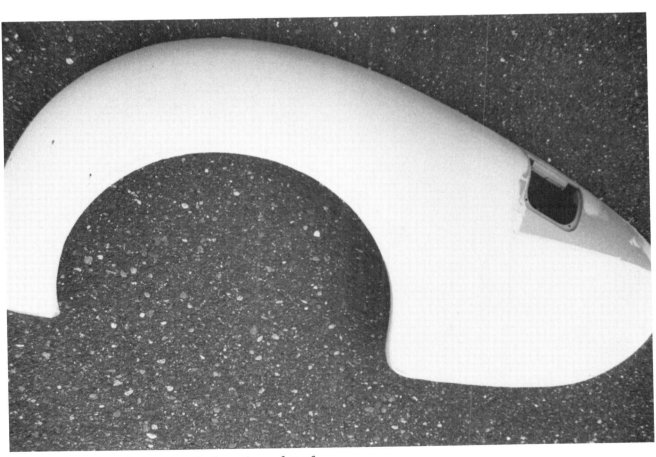

The second coat is applied to virtually the entire surface of the fender.

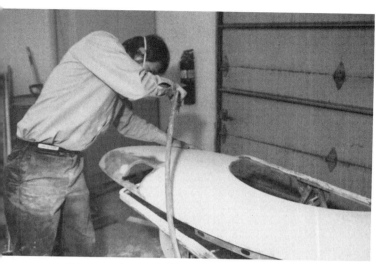

The second coat of filler is sanded first with the 36 grit pad and then with the 80 grit pad on the mud hog. Ron blows the dust off the fender and inspects it for pin holes or imperfections in the filler.

The media is recycled, filtered, and used over again, until it gets too pulverized to cut the paint. In fact, new media is seldom used alone; some old media is usually mixed with the new in order to dampen the cutting action. Because the old media and paint dust contain no toxic chemicals (the small amount of lead in some old paint pigments is considered insignificant), disposal of the dust is never a problem and helps to hold down the cost of the process.

When you consider the high cost, mess, and environmental problems inherent in chemically stripping a body, this new plastic blasting looks pretty good. It costs no more than chemically stripping a part; it's neater, safer, less toxic, and leaves no stripping residue in nooks and crannies where it can seep out later and ruin a new paint job. If you've got rust to deal with, then this is not the best method. But if you're just trying to get off the old paint, taking it to a shop that uses plastic media to remove paint makes all the sense in the world.

Strip Rite is located in a suburb of Minneapolis. In other parts of the country, a shop can be located by call-

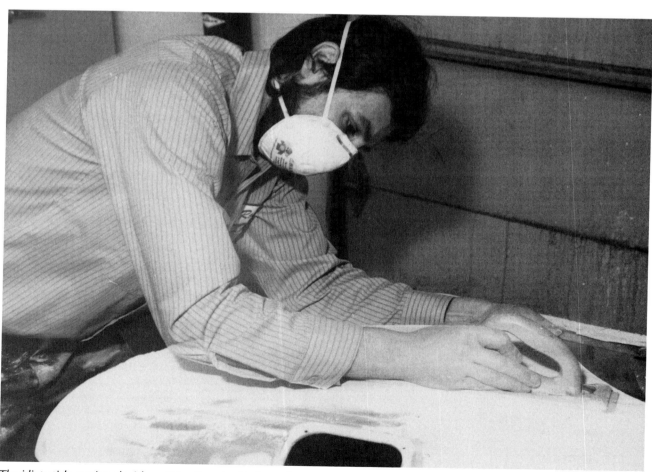

The idiot stick, equipped with an 80 grit pad, aids in getting the lower part of the fender flat. The more rounded parts of the fender are sanded with a flexible sanding pad.

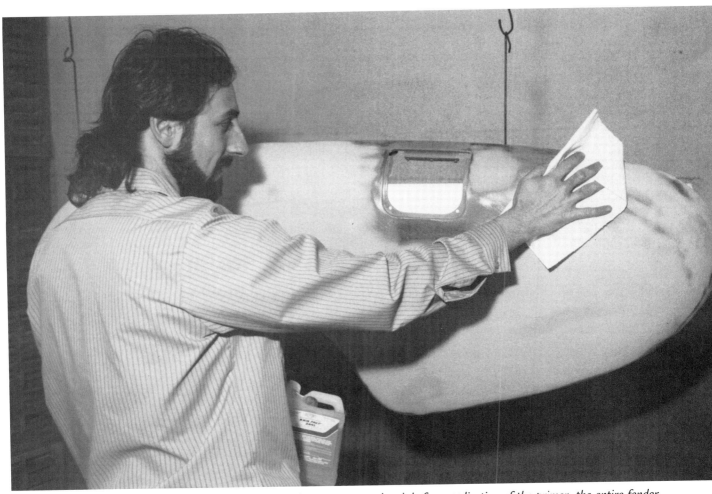

After sanding the second coat of filler, first with the mud hog and then by hand, the fender has a pretty good shape and Ron decides to proceed to the next step in the finishing sequence, primer-surfacer. Bare metal spots are treated with metal etch before application of the primer, the entire fender is then wiped off with wax and grease remover and then a tack rag.

ing the Dry Stripping Facilities Network (an industry group). They will direct you to the nearest dry stripping specialist. See the Sources section for the phone number of Strip Rite and the DSFN.

Dip Stripping

If you can't eliminate the rust with sandblasting, what can you do to get the rust off that old body? Dip stripping might be the answer. This type of stripping, where the entire body or basket of parts is lowered into a bath of some kind, breaks down into two very different methods: acid dipping and electrochemical stripping.

Acid Dipping

Acid dipping is just what the name implies, an acid bath for your rusty parts. The acid removes rust but it also removes some of the good metal as well, a nondiscriminatory method, so to speak. Thus it becomes dangerous to take in the door from the Model A with the

rust perforation along the bottom edge, as there might not be much door skin left when it comes out of the bath. The other problem with the acid dip is the effect of residual acid, left behind in pinch welds and crevices, on new paint. Another potential problem is the fact that the acid can cause embrittlement of the steel.

A better dip strip method involves a two-part, nonacid bath, known as electrochemical or electrolytic cleaning. This noncorrosive process will remove paint and rust without attacking any of the good metal.

Electrochemical Dipping

Known as electrochemical cleaning, this two-step process will remove the rust, all the rust, and only the rust from that old coupe body. Holes that were the size of a quarter when you brought the body in will be exactly the same size when you take the body home. The only difference is that the rust around that hole will be gone completely.

The first step of the process is a caustic bath. Individual parts are loaded into baskets, bodies are suspended by special fixtures, and they are dipped in a large tank of caustic liquid. This first step will loosen all paint, dirt, and grease. After the parts come out of the first bath, they are washed off with high-pressure hoses. This high-pressure spray—3,000psi—is what actually takes off the softened paint and grease. Typical parts stay in the first solution overnight; if the paint is extra thick, then it takes a little longer. Areas filled with lead or plastic filler may need to be worked over with a putty knife to help the solution work down to bare metal.

Step two is where the action really starts—with a little help from some DC electricity. The parts are immersed in an alkaline solution, one with plenty of hydroxyl (HO) ions in it. Chemically, rust is iron oxide, Fe_2O_3, formed when iron mixes with oxygen. Water speeds this process by providing a conductor between the iron and the oxygen. Salt increases the conductivity of water and thus further speeds the rusting process.

Let's go back to our parts in the second step of the skinny-dipping process. The rusty body is immersed in the alkaline solution, then a DC current is run between the body and the solution. By making the body the positive pole and immersing the negative pole in the solution, an electron is induced to move from a hydroxyl ion and attach itself to the iron oxide (or rust) molecules. When this extra electron combines with the iron oxide, the bond between the iron and the oxygen is broken. The oxygen now floats up to the surface (helping to scrub the parts clean as it does) and the iron is released into the solution. The unrusted steel is unaffected by this process.

Occasionally the polarity of the process is reversed, which makes the body the negative pole. During this reversal period hydrogen (H_2) is released from the mixture. The hydrogen bubbles help to scrub the body (much like the oxygen did earlier), and the reversed polarity helps to repel dirt from the body.

How long does all this take? Typical immersion times for the second step range from overnight for light rust, to three or four days for heavy accumulations of rust.

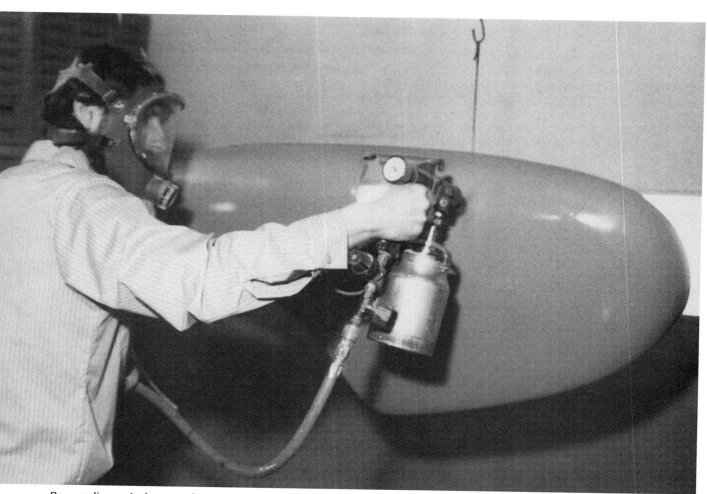

Ron applies a single coat of two-part primer (DP 50) and then three coats of primer-surfacer.

When the primer-surfacer has dried completely, Ron puts on a very light coat of dark lacquer primer to act as a guide coat during the block sanding to follow.

Block sanding the primer-surfacer starts with 120 grit paper on a flexible pad.

Ron keeps the pad flat on the fender and works the entire surface. The primer-surfacer is used to fill the 80 grit scratches left from the last step—this block sanding will eliminate the high spots and show up any lingering low spots.

This is a close up of the fender after block sanding with 120 grit. Dark areas show up small low spots where the guide coat was not sanded off.

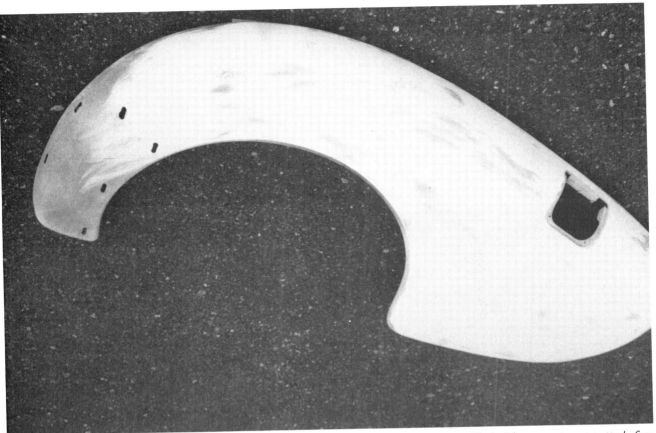

Overview of the fender after the first block sanding with 120 grit shows a number of small low spots—small enough to be filled with the next application of primer-surfacer. Larger low spots would need to be filled with two-part spot putty before the fender got the second coat of primer-surfacer.

When the rust is all gone, the parts are removed from the tank and given one final rinse. Then everything is coated with a light phosphate solution to prevent flash-rusting until painting.

Russ Pastorious of International Metal Stripping, St. Paul, Minnesota, stressed the fact that parts and bodies need to be completely disassembled so the solutions can get at all the nooks and crannies. "Sometimes people bring in doors with the regulators still inside or a chassis with the suspension components still intact. The other thing that takes a lot of time is removing undercoating and seam sealers. Guys want to know what they can do to make the job easier and a little cheaper. Well, they should completely disassemble everything, and if they want to take off as much undercoat as possible at home, that will make our job easier."

Though it isn't cheap, electrochemical cleaning is the best, most thorough cleaning method for any rusty parts. Real world costs start at $1,200-$1,700 for a complete early sedan body. A late-model unibody car like a Road-runner might run as high as $2,500-$3,000, depending again on the condition. Dipping a complete early-style frame runs from $250-$300; fully boxed frames contain a

Here are a couple of old Model A fenders, with very heavy rust on the back side. Getting the paint off won't be hard, the rust however is another story.

57

lot more material and cost somewhat more to dip.

For a real world examination of the process, I let Russ strip one of the Model A fenders. Though the paint wasn't very thick, the rust was, especially on the back side. The first step, in the caustic tank, only took overnight to loosen all the remaining paint. Step two, in the rust removal tank, took a little longer due to the heavy rust on the back side of the parts. The second step took almost a week to completely eliminate the rust from the deep pits in the back side of the fender.

Electrochemical stripping is not cheap, it's not easy,

Russ Pastorius, owner of International Metal Stripping, loads the Model A fender into a basket. The first step in the stripping process is the caustic tank where the paint is softened.

but it is just about the only game in town if the rust is extensive. It won't weaken or embrittle the metal, and it won't leave behind acid residues to ruin your new paint job. If you're looking for a facility that does electrochemical stripping, you will just have to check the phone book, ask at the local shops, and see who advertises in the local street-rodding newsletter.

Chemical Stripping

If the part you're trying to strip is smaller than a five-nine Caddy and there isn't any (or at least not much) rust, then you may want to strip it at home. A variety of paint strippers are available at the hardware or paint supply store. Most will remove nearly any type of paint. Anyone who thinks this process is easy (even on small parts) either hasn't tried it yet or spent too much time with their nose in a can of lacquer thinner. Chemically stripping even small parts is a time-consuming job, a messy operation that requires rubber gloves, an apron, and good ventilation.

Most of the strippers qualify as toxic waste. If you use very much of the materials, you should take the time to dispose of them responsibly (see the disposal section at the back of the book). In order to avoid the disposal hassle, you should use one of the new, environmentally friendly strippers.

If what you're trying to do is take off the old paint because it's too thick or you simply want to start from bare metal, then one of these liquid strippers might be right for the job. Each brand of stripper will have a slightly different set of directions—be sure to take the time to read them. Most recommend that you score the surface with a razor blade for example, to help the stripper get

After spending the night in the caustic tank the fender is pulled out and sprayed off with high pressure water.

under the surface of the paint to work faster.

Most can be brushed on with an old paint brush. By moving the brush in one direction, the stripper will "glaze over" with an agent in the stripper that prevents it from drying out. If you brush back and forth, this anti-drying agent is rendered useless.

The paint stripper works best if you leave it alone and give the chemicals time to work. Two or three applications are often necessary and will still require some hand work with sandpaper at edges and crevices after the stripper is all removed. Be sure to clean the parts thoroughly after the last coat of stripper and follow the directions with regard to any final flushing procedures. At the very least, wash the parts down with lacquer thinner or a similar cleanser so there's no lingering stripper to react

with and ruin the new paint.

It's often a good idea to use a metal prep or metal etch agent prior to the first application of primer. Strippers usually leave steel in a poor condition to bond with the first coat of paint. Again, each of these products is a little different. Some are one-step products and some require two steps. Take the time to read and follow the directions.

Sanding

Sanding is certainly a less than ideal means of stripping parts. It's time consuming, expensive, and dirty. It works reasonably well if the parts aren't too big, the paint isn't too thick, and there isn't much rust.

Though it sounds obvious, always sand with a pad

The next step for the Model A fender is the rust removal tank. An elaborate system of overhead winches makes it easy to move the baskets from tank to tank. After nearly a week in the rust removal tank, the fender comes out for a final *rinse and inspection. How long it takes to eliminate the rust depends on how heavy the rust is and the size and shape of the part.*

The tanks at International Metal Striping are big enough to immerse a complete body like this 1957 Ford.

Plastic blasting is done in a large "spray booth" so all the dust is contained. Everything from complete cars to smaller parts made from steel, aluminum or fiberglass can be safely stripped.

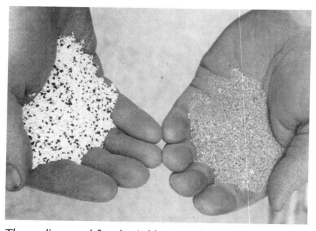

The medium used for plastic blasting is little bits of thermoset plastic. On the left, looking like some powdered detergent with magic bleach crystals, are the fresh beads of plastic. On the right are the worn-out beads after a number of passes through the gun. A good operator has a great deal of control—and can in fact take paint off one layer at a time. The bits of plastic ride a column of air running at 20-40psi (usually more like 20).

no more aggressive than necessary, and use a D-A instead of a big grinder. When doing any kind of bodywork or sanding it's good to remember that large grinders create lots of heat (which work-harden and warp the metal), and a coarse pad creates grooves that need to be filled later.

If the rust is minor, there are some gels available from the hardware store or the paint supply house that you apply after the rust is sanded as best you can. The gel is then applied and allowed to dry. The liquid turns black as it reacts with the rust and dries. After drying, the surface looks like dried epoxy resin and can be sanded and painted. These products don't eliminate the rust, rather they make them chemically inert. This is not the answer for large panels or complete bodies, but it might work for small areas when no other means is readily available.

Finally...

The method you use to strip the paint and crud from that old body is going to depend on your pocketbook, the resources available to you, and your personal preference. Electrochemical cleaning is one of the best rust removal methods available, though it can be hard to find a facility in some parts of the country. Plastic blasting does a great job on paint while leaving the metal—and rust—just as they were. Acid dips and chemical strippers pose a series of problems that make them less than ideal for all but small parts or special situations.

In the end you need to use a system that's neat and doesn't trouble your conscience when you stuff the remains in the garbage can. Pick a system that doesn't leave behind traces of chemicals that cause a paint failure later. More than anything, find a system that won't damage that precious iron you're trying so hard to save.

This Chevy truck cab has already been through the booth. Note that the paint is gone, yet the filler on the fender has been left intact.

Interview: Doug Thompson

Doug Thompson has been building custom cars and hot rods for more than thirty years. Doug is probably best known to street-rodders as the builder of the "String of Pearls" '41 Ford convertible; the radical Packard "Evening Shadows," built for Richard Ratty; and the Hirohata Merc clone owned by Jack Walker. Anyone who's seen the '41 Ford convert will agree that Doug is a man who understands how to create a wonderful paint job. The Ford looks blue, until you hit the right angle, and then it shows lavender light reflected by the pearl flakes. Doug says that he uses a lot of material and disregards the warnings regarding film thickness. I don't know exactly how thick the paint on the Ford is, but it has that look of a pool—one that's apparently deep enough to swim in.

Doug, let's start with you, your background, and how you learned to paint.

Well, even as a kid, I wanted to build glamorous display or show cars. Now the trouble I had is that the people selling paints go by acceptable tolerances. These people are in the repair business, so their objectives are different from a customizer's goals. Most of the stuff I learned early on I learned from a guy who worked for a casket manufacturer before he got involved with cars. The whole concept is different when you're painting a casket. It needs to look top notch, beautiful, and expensive, one time. Then they put it in the ground. The cars I built were mostly show cars anyway, so I wasn't real concerned with longevity and fading under sunlight and that kind of thing, so the concept worked real well for me. This meant forgetting film thickness and compatibility and all the things that the paint store told you. We took materials and we played with them, we experimented. Of course I eventually learned the importance of limiting film thickness, but because of that early experience I never allowed worries about maximum thickness or paint specs to scare me into sacrificing the looks of a job.

As time went on I learned what wouldn't last very long and what would. Some of the early candies were nitrocellulose lacquers; they would last only a year in the sunlight. The acrylic lacquers that came later were better, they didn't crack, but they would fade pretty bad because the dyes weren't real strong.

When I had something that I thought looked good, that is what I used. I began using light bulbs for testing colors and making display samples. The advantage being there is no prep, all the samples look the same, and the curvature of the bulb shows highlights easily. It worked much better than scrap metal and was easier because scrap metal needs some prep before you can paint it.

Tell us more about some of your painting techniques.

Well, I still do mostly lacquer jobs, and I spray the layers as quickly as I can so that the layers all bond into one film. Primer and fillers, however, I like to let sit as long as I can so they shrink as much as possible.

How did you get that nice pearl effect on the '41 Ford convertible?

The pearl is a series of small flat flakes that look like little coins or leaves. Because of the way they're made, you can get very different effects from different mixes of the same material. For example, you can take a 1 gallon (gal) can and put in 1 quart (qt) of clear and then add 1lb of pearl. Now you've got a paste. You can thin that until you've got one full gallon. Now when it comes out of the gun, it goes on the surface like a satin finish aluminum because all the platelets are overlapping. The clear is real thin—there isn't much suspension—so all the platelets sink quick and they lay flat, so they all reflect the same way from the same direction.

The other extreme would be to take a 1gal can, you put 3qt of clear, and 1/4lb of pearl, and then thin it to make the same viscosity. Now you spray it on and you hardly see any pearl at all. You look at it and you're looking through it. So many coats are required to get the same amount of pearl on the surface. There's a couple of other options here too. If you use slow dry reducer, then the flakes are still moving as they sink, like leaves falling off the tree. Whichever angle they set up in is the angle they reflect light from. If you spray a lot of coats of pearl like this, coat upon coat, with lots of these little things suspended in there at different angles, then it really looks like a pearl.

Now, if you use just a little pearl in a lot of clear and thin or reduce it to dry fast, then they all set up at the same angle. This gives you a strong pearl effect, or flash, that happens because of that angle. When the sun hits the '41 Ford at that certain angle, the pearl lights up. I'm not sure the people who manufacture this stuff understand all the things you can do with it.

So you sprayed dry coats of pearl mix on top of the blue basecoat, and then added some wet clearcoats on top to give the '41 Ford that wonderful shine?

Yes, a lot of the new base colors don't have any shine, they get the shine from the clearcoat. So that's what I did with the pearl layers. All those coats didn't have much shine, but then I put some wet clearcoats on top to give the car that deep luster.

When working with candy paints you can get a lot of different effects depending on whether or not you blend the base and candy or separate them. For example, let's say you were shooting candy red over silver. If you shoot the silver, get good coverage, and then maybe you sand the silver lightly (depending on the recommendations of the manufacturer), and now you're ready for the candycoat. You've got some silver left in the mixing can. You can leave the silver in there as you mix the red candy and shoot it that way. Each time you leave the remains in the can. If you do it this way you get more of a pearl effect, less of the classic candy look. All I'm trying to say is there's more than one way to do candies or pearls.

I think most of the guys who are really good at painting have learned a lot of these and other little tricks over the years, sometimes by accident. The truth is there's a wide range of possibilities you can get from a certain set of materials.

Is that why you use light bulbs, because they make it easier to check the results from different techniques?

Yes, I can put twelve bulbs in a piece of cardboard and try twelve different methods or colors and then walk outside and see which one gives me the effect I want. The bulbs can make a nice display too and help you to sell a job or sell your skills to the next customer.

How do you pick a particular color for a car you build?

Sometimes the customer already has a color in mind. I spray up several colors, including my choice, and together we imagine the color best suited to the car. I consider the brightest colors to be performance oriented, and the neutral and darker colors to be comfort and luxury oriented. I think candies and pearls are particularly suited to cars with lots of compound curves, mainly because you get more highlights.

What difference do you see in people starting out painting today, compared with the days when you were growing up?

What's different is that they're scared. I suppose they've been taught to be scared. They're afraid to experiment. When you buy a gallon of paint, there's four sheets of technical information you have to read before you can use the paint. How are you going to be creative with a system like that? When I was a kid there wasn't any of that; you just bought the paint and did it. When I go up to buy urethane, and I've got to read all

A big believer in the creative use of painting materials, Doug Thompson from Kansas City, Missouri, has been building and painting custom cars since high school.

this stuff—maybe that's why I haven't used much of the modern materials. I sprayed two of our own vehicles with urethane, and they seem pretty durable. But I feel limited when I use the materials because I'm given all these warnings about the specs, and I'm warned repeatedly about how toxic the materials are. And I realize these warnings are not to be taken lightly.

I'm a big believer in apprenticeship. I think if a person wants to get real good, it helps to learn from someone who's done it. Based on my own career, I didn't just buy the equipment, I searched out a bodyshop and explained that I would sweep the floors and do the dirty jobs if I could watch them paint. You can learn a lot from someone who's good at what he or she does if they're willing to share it and you're willing to listen.

Chapter 5

A Modern Paint Job Done
With Modern Materials

The paint job seen in this chapter was applied at Twin Town Street Rods in St. Paul, Minnesota, by Jeff Stanke. This chapter documents each step of that paint job, starting with the primer-surfacer stage, and following along all the way to the clearcoat. The car is a 1931 Model A coupe belonging to Dan Larsen of St. Paul,

This is where we start, with a Model A body at Twin Town Street Rods in St. Paul, Minnesota. The metal work and body work have already been finished. What's left is some final prep work before applying the final color.

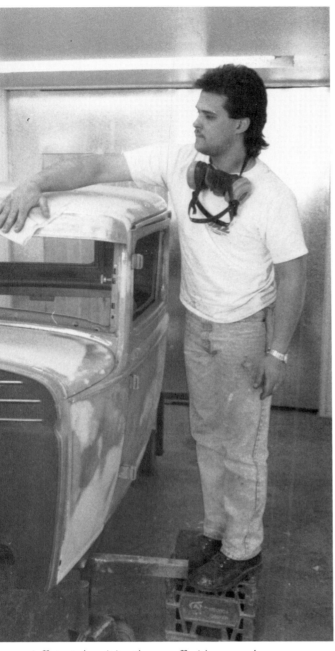

Jeff starts by wiping the car off with wax and grease remover and then with a tack rag, before applying a sealer coat.

Jeff begins application of the sealer (DP 50 in this case) on the left side of the roof and follows a logical pattern as he works his way around the car.

Minnesota. The paint is a PPG product, a two-step, basecoat-clearcoat product.

Preparation

By preparation we mean the work that is done after the filler is applied and before the finished paint is applied to the car. Careful preparation is necessary to create really flat, smooth panels, panels that will show a good gloss after the topcoats are applied.

When Jeff is finished with the metalwork on the

Model A and has all the plastic filler smoothed to his satisfaction (see the third book in this series, *How To Do Hot Rod Bodywork*, for more on metalwork and the use of fillers) he begins to prepare for the finished paint by applying a uniform coat of DP 50 (this is the light gray-colored DP product) epoxy primer from PPG. The DP 50 is being used as a sealer and also as a good base for the primer-surfacer coat to follow. Before spraying the DP 50 paint Jeff first wipes the car down with wax and grease remover and then a tack rag.

The two-part primer is mixed per the instructions on the can. Jeff applies one good coat, being careful to get the paint into all the nooks and crannies of the car, and then allows the two-part primer to dry for one hour before applying the primer-surfacer.

The primer-surfacer Jeff uses is Prima (also known as K 36) from the PPG line. As mentioned earlier, primer-surfacers are used to fill scratches left in the underlying layers of metal or filler material by fairly coarse paper like 36 or 80 grit. Application of the primer-surfacer and

Next he sprays the right side of the roof. Note how Jeff holds the hose so it doesn't contact the body. Before finishing with the sealer coat, Jeff gets paint into the door jamb areas and all the little nooks and crannies.

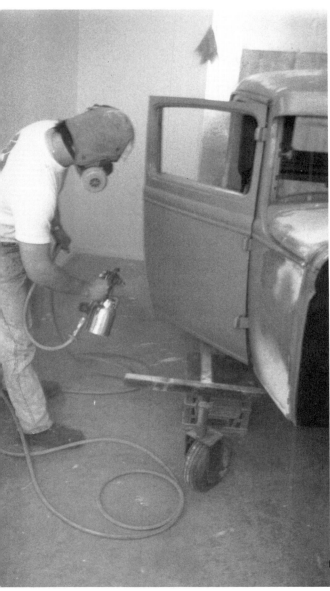

The door is sprayed in a series of horizontal passes, with each new pass overlapping the last by 50 percent.

some careful block sanding will fill all the scratches and leave a perfectly smooth, flat surface so the finish paint shows no scratches, lays down flat, and has maximum gloss.

Before spraying the primer-surfacer, Jeff carefully cleans the gun and explains, "The new epoxy-type primers are great, but if you leave them in the gun too long they set up in the gun, which means you can't get the gun clean."

Jeff applies three coats of the primer-surfacer, waiting for 20 minutes between each coat for the material to flash. The idea is to leave enough material on the car so that you can block-sand some off. Because the three

A clean gun is essential for good paint application. And with the new two-part primers and paints, if they harden in the gun, you get to buy a new one.

coats leave quite a bit of material on the car, Jeff allows the primer-surfacer to dry for a full 24 hours to be sure that it shrinks fully before sanding the surface.

Before he begins to block sand the primer-surfacer, Jeff applies a guide coat. As mentioned, this is just a light coat of primer in a contrasting color (often lacquer primer is used here) that makes it easy to see the low spots left in the panels.

The guide coat dries almost immediately, and Jeff starts block sanding the entire car with 120 grit paper. The sanding block Jeff uses depends on the panel he's working on. For large panels like the doors or the roof, Jeff uses a long idiot stick; smaller panels get a shorter pad while on the curves he uses a very flexible foam pad.

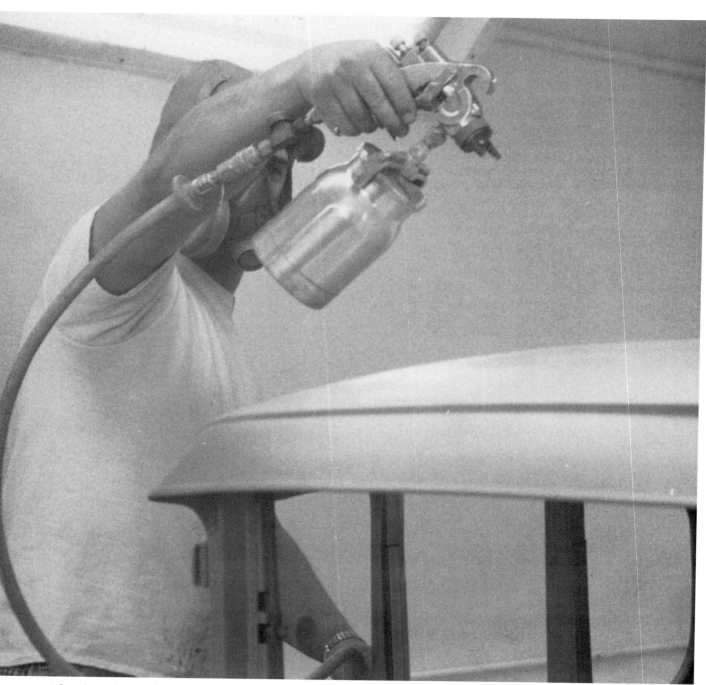

After the sealer has dried for one hour (dry times are different for different sealer products) Jeff begins the first application of the primer-surfacer. The primer-surfacer used here is Prima (K-36) from PPG. This is a good two-part product that is mixed with the correct reducer (depending on the temperature in the booth) and the K 201 hardener.

Block sanding of the area below the trunk lid shows a sizable low spot, one too big to be filled by the next applications of primer-surfacer. Jeff mixes up some polyester glazing putty, often known as "spot putty." Jeff advises that any spot putty you use "should be a two-part putty; they're a lot stronger and shrink less than the earlier one-part putties. The nice thing about using spot putty is you can put it down over paint, unlike regular body filler, which needs to be applied over bare metal or a two-part primer."

The spot putty is applied much as you would regular body filler. Jeff is quick to apply the putty after mix-

Once again, Jeff works his way around the car, being careful to keep the gun perpendicular to the surface and the hose away from the body. The primer-surfacer is applied in three coats, with a twenty minute flash time between each coat. The idea is to leave enough material on the car to fill sand scratches and small low spots.

The primer-surfacer is applied to the door in a series of horizontal passes. Note that as Jeff moves toward the camera the spray gun is moved in a horizontal line and that the spray pattern overlaps the last pass by about 50 percent.

ing it, as it sets up faster than regular body filler. After the putty has set up, Jeff sands it with 120 grit paper (the same grit he was using on the primer surfacer). To ensure that this area blends with the rest of the car, Jeff applies three more coats of primer-surfacer, allows them to dry, and then block sands the area one more time.

After the entire car is block sanded and any low spots filled, Jeff blows loose dust off the car with compressed air, wipes it down with a tack rag, and applies three more coats of primer-surfacer, waiting 20 minutes between each coat for the paint to flash. Again, Jeff waits 24 hours so the primer-surfacer will shrink fully

before he starts block sanding.

The next block sanding operation is done with 400 grit paper. Jeff applies another guide coat, though some painters would skip the guide coat for the second block sanding operation. The entire car is block sanded with 400 grit paper that is kept wet throughout the entire process. What Jeff is doing is filling the 120 grit sanding scratches left from the last step of the operation and further flattening the body panels. At this point, using too soft a pad and sanding with too much effort can put lumps in the primer surfacer. So Jeff uses a fairly stiff pad and sands only enough to fill the sand scratches and knock down any obvious high spots.

After three coats of primer-surfacer the old coupe is almost ready for block sanding, there's just one more thing.

70

Here Jeff applies a guide coat in a dark color to aid in finding any low spots.

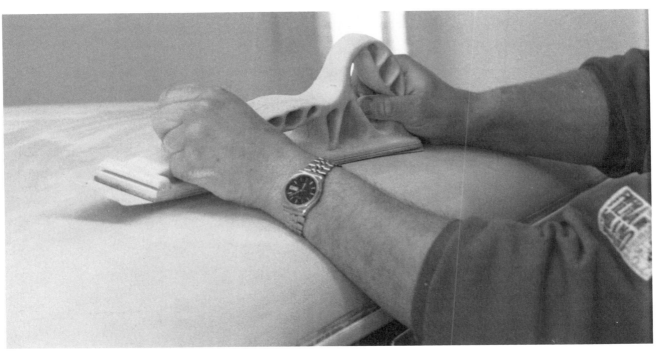

Block sanding is usually done in stages using a variety of blocks. For large flat areas like the roof and door, Jeff uses this long "idiot stick" and self-adhering sand paper. Block sanding must be done in a crisscross pattern so as not to sand flat ridges into the primer-surfacer.

Following the wet sanding of the entire car with 400 grit, Jeff wipes off the body and gives everything a close examination. A few small holes are discovered—and filled with spot putty. After the putty sets up, it is block sanded with wet, 400 grit paper.

As a general rule, if the rest of the car is ready for sealer and final paint, and only small areas were spot puttied, then those areas can be block sanded and sealed without first applying another coat of primer-surfacer. When the area is large, however, sanding the putty should be followed by another application of primer-surfacer before the sealer is applied.

In most cases the application of sealer and final paint needs to be coordinated so the final paint is applied during the correct window of time. Jeff likes to use a two-part primer from PPG for a sealer (check the product information sheet because not all primer products can be used as a sealer). In the case of the Model A, the car is wiped down with wax and grease remover, and wiped down with a tack rag before application of the DP 50.

The color used on the Model A is bright aqua poly, a 1993 GM color. This is a basecoat-clearcoat situation, where the gloss is created by the clearcoat.

Jeff points out that, "When you spray a color that's a basecoat-clearcoat system, the basecoat goes on flat. If you spray it so it's real glossy, you've probably put on too much paint. I always mix all the basecoat, or colored paint into one can, and then fill the paint gun from that can. That way I'm sure that when I come to

Smaller areas require smaller blocks, curved panels are sanded with small flexible pads.

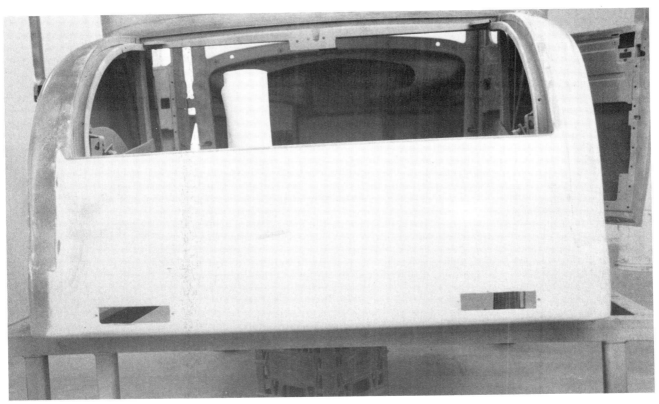

After block sanding the area below the trunk lid a series of small low spots show up.

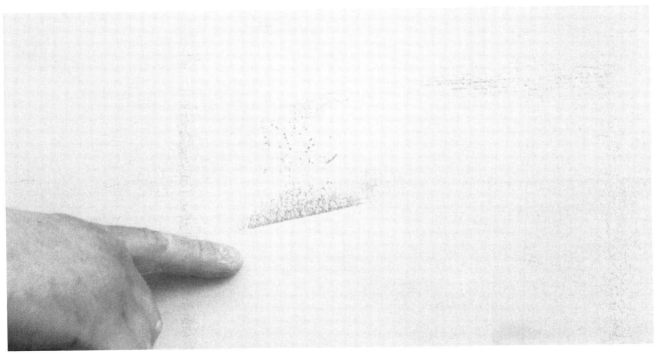

This close up shows the dark primer that remains in the low area and makes it easy to see. Areas like these are filled with two-part spot putty.

The two-part spot putty is mixed much like the more common body filler. Jeff notes that the material sets up fast so it must be applied immediately.

After mixing the spot putty it is applied with a small flexible paddle. If you're careful only one application will be needed.

do the fenders later I don't end up with a slightly different color. And if I buy two or more gallons of paint, I make sure it all has the same lot number for the same reason."

It's almost time to spray the final colors, but first Jeff goes over the entire car with a tube of sealer in a caulk gun. The idea is to fill the tiny cracks where panels meet or on the underside of the rain gutter along the roof.

After spraying on a medium coat of DP 50 to act as the sealer, Jeff waits 1 hour before applying the first basecoat. Jeff puts the first coat on a little light, so it will act as a "tack coat" and help the adhesion of the heavier coats to follow. In total, Jeff puts on four coats of the basecoat, waiting 20 minutes between coats, using a conventional high-pressure gun running on 40-50lb at the gun with the trigger pulled.

After drying, the puttied areas are block sanded with the same 120 grit paper that was used on the surrounding primer-surfacer. Block sanding continues until the filled areas feel just right to Jeff's experienced hand.

One hour after applying the last basecoat, Jeff begins applying the multiple coats of clearcoat. It's important to note that with basecoat-clearcoat systems, no sanding or polishing is ever done on the color, it's always done on the clearcoat. For that reason, Jeff puts four coats of urethane clear on the car, knowing that there's plenty of clear to polish without any danger of rubbing through.

After allowing the last clearcoat to dry for at least 24 hours, Jeff starts in on the polishing operation. "Find a system you're comfortable with," is Jeff's advice. "Stick with it and follow the directions that come with the product."

Jeff uses a 3M system, one that recommends beginning with 1,200 grit sandpaper and ends with 3M Finesse-It polish. Jeff uses a fairly stiff sanding block and a

lot of water as he starts in with the 1,200 grit sandpaper. It's important that the back side of the block be perfectly clean and flat. Even a small bit of sand between the paper and the block will cause a high spot in the paper and a resulting groove in the paint.

Jeff starts out with a fairly stiff sanding block equipped with a piece of 1,200 grit sandpaper. The motions he uses are circular, to avoid rubbing grooves or ridges into the panels, and he is careful to keep the paper very wet during the process. The water helps to keep the paper cool and also flushes away sanding debris.

With the 1,200 grit paper, Jeff flattens the clearcoat, eliminating the subtle orange peel effect. It's important to note that the actual flattening is done

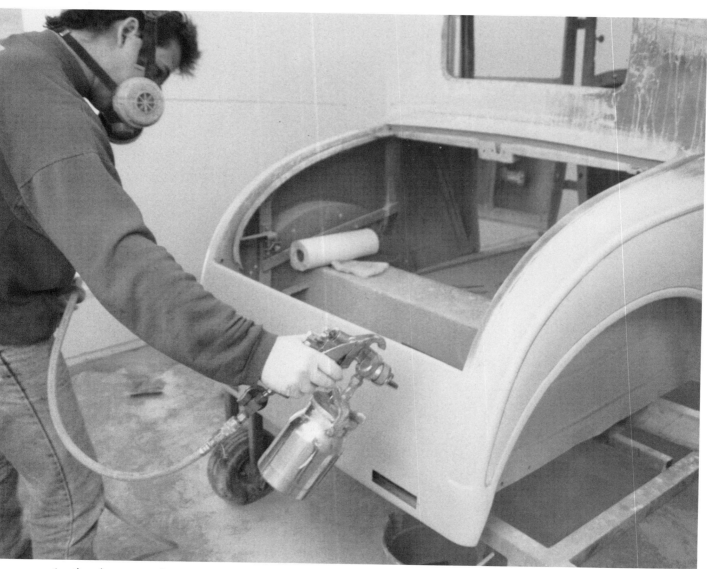

Another three coats of primer-surfacer are applied to the puttied areas and then block sanded. When the entire car has been block sanded and any low spots filled, Jeff will apply another three coats of primer-surfacer.

After Jeff has applied another three coats of primer-surfacer and allowed them to dry for twenty-four hours, he puts on another guide coat before starting the final block sanding.

The final block sanding is done with 400 grit paper and soapy water. This operation will eliminate sanding scratches left from the 120 grit paper and further flatten the panels.

with the 1,200 grit; the finer grit paper and polish that follow are used primarily to eliminate the scratches left by the 1,200 grit paper.

Jeff applies the last clearcoat fairly heavy and wet, in order to produce maximum gloss. It is this heavy layer of clear that he sands into with the circular motion.

When the entire car has been wet sanded with the 1,200 grit and the little hills and valleys have been eliminated from the clearcoat, Jeff changes to 1,500 paper (some people go to 2,000 grit) and uses circular motions to eliminate the scratches left by the earlier 1,200 grit sanding. Jeff is careful to wash and wipe down the entire

Jeff starts sanding on the cowl, keeping the paper wet as he moves along. The entire car will be sanded in this way. The next step is sealer and then final paint.

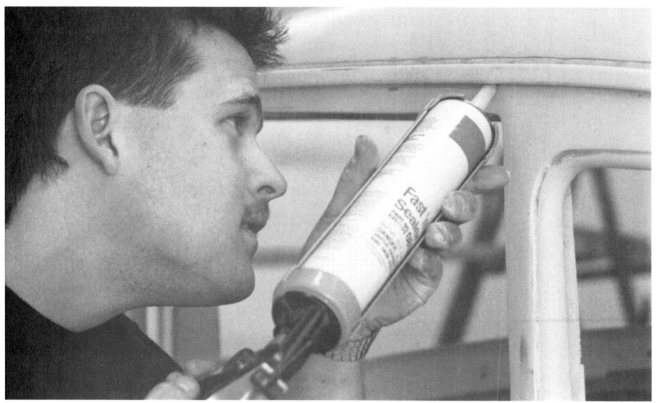

A variety of caulk-type sealers are available to seal small seams before the final paint is applied. Here Jeff puts a nice smooth bead along the bottom of the rain gutter where it meets the body.

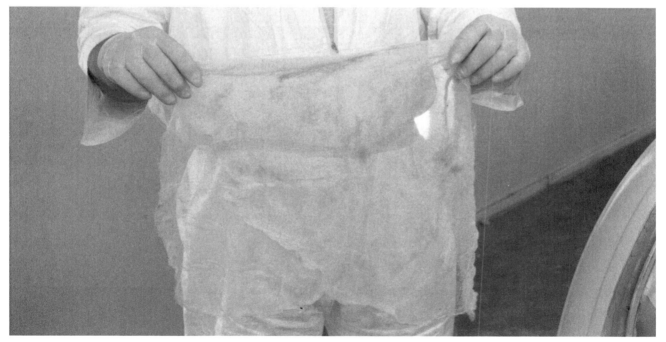

After blowing off any dust and wiping the car down with wax and grease remover, Jeff takes a new tack rag and allows it to "air" before using it on the car.

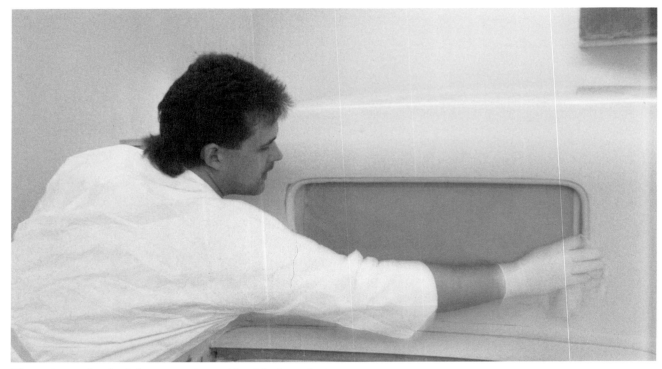

The entire car is wiped down very thoroughly with the tack rag before application of the sealer coat.

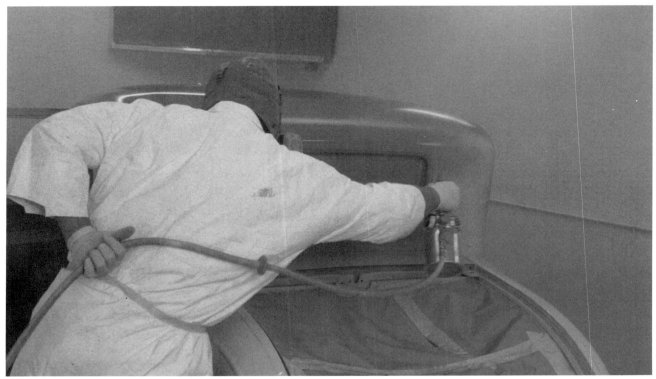

Jeff begins the application of the sealer coat (DP 50 in this case), being careful to apply the paint in a nice even coat because it won't be sanded before the basecoats are applied.

The complete painter's suit will ensure that Jeff is protected from the paint and that the paint job will not pick up any dust from Jeff's clothes.

car between each of the sanding/polishing operations to ensure that there is no residue left on the car that might get caught under the sandpaper and cut grooves in the paint job—the idea here is to smooth the paint, not put more scratches in it.

During this whole color sanding operation, the entire car is kept closed up with masking paper, as it makes the later job of cleanup much easier.

The 3M polishing compound comes in two grades and is known as Finesse-It. The system includes both the compound and different pads for use with the different compounds.

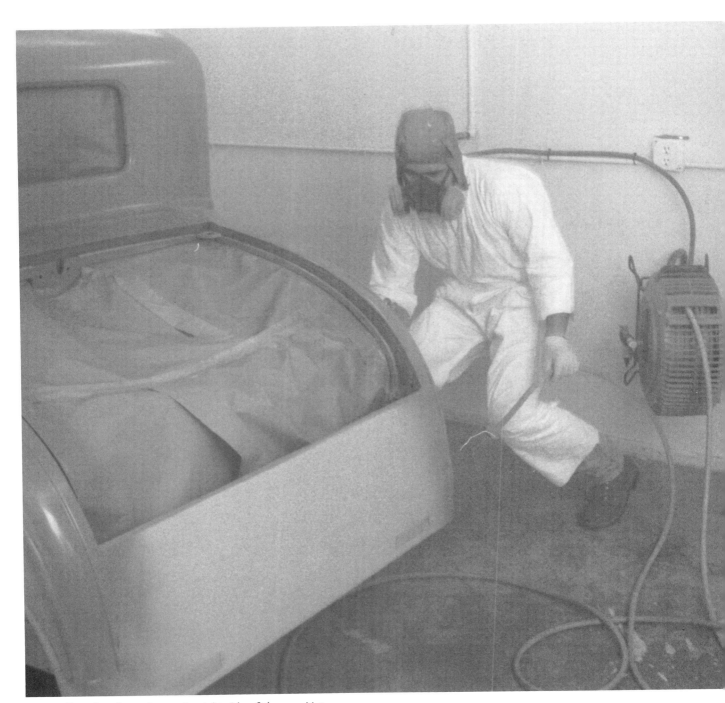

Here Jeff applies the sealer to the right side of the car. Note the complete painter's suit and gloves. Note the large reel for the air hose, which leaves less of the hose lying on the cold concrete floor.

After cleaning the car from the last operation, Jeff puts the correct foam pad on the electric buffer and applies the coarser compound to the panel he intends to polish. Jeff likes the foam pads and feels they are especially good for beginners because, "you wet the pad first, and it always holds a little water, which helps to keep it cool. The pads are really good for beginners; they don't bunch up like the wool pads do."

Jeff works one small area at a time, stopping often to inspect the finish. If the surface is still cloudy and contains scratches, then he goes over it again with the same compound before moving on to a new area. 3M recommends that the buffer speed be kept between 1,500 and 2,500 (slower is better, especially for beginners) and that

Here's the coupe with the complete sealer coat before application of the color. The sealer makes the entire body one uniform color, prevents any interaction between the primer and final coats, and provides good color hold out.

the pad be kept flat against the panel if possible.

Jeff suggests that, "Beginners should start on a flat panel, because it's harder to get in trouble and burn the paint there. It also helps to have a lot of light for the polishing so you can really see what you're doing. When I come to a curve or the edge of a panel, I just don't spend much time there, it's just too easy to burn through."

For the final step, Jeff likes to use a one-step wax or glaze product. His personal favorite is Liquid Lustre, as it seems to contain a glaze that melts into the paint to fill tiny scratches. It's not a good idea to seal the new paint surface with a sealer or poly-type product, as the paint needs to breathe after application. Jeff also advises against the use of products that contain silicone because the silicone can cause fish-eyes and other problems with paint jobs that are performed later.

Paint the Fenders

In the case of the Model A, the fenders are fiberglass units from Wescott's. (Anyone painting fiberglass should read the recommendations contained in chapter 4.) These fenders arrived in pretty good condition, so the amount of finishing work was minimal. Jeff feels that, "If the fenders need a lot of finish work or repair, it should be done on the car or a good fixture, so the fender doesn't take on a new shape while you're working on it."

Rather than mix paint for the body and then later mix more paint for the fenders, Jeff mixes enough basecoat paint to do the entire car—so all the paint is exactly the same color.

After the sealer coat is dry, Jeff inspects the paint job for imperfections and then wipes it down with a tack rag again.

After four coats of basecoat the body has a dull shine. The actual gloss is provided by the clearcoats to follow. Basecoats like this are not sanded or polished, that is done on the clearcoat.

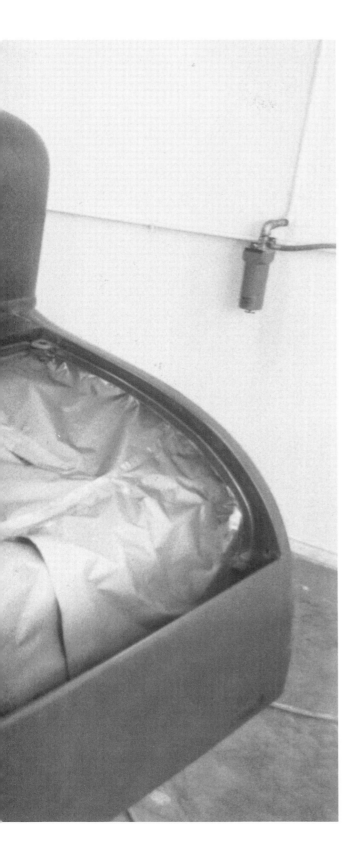

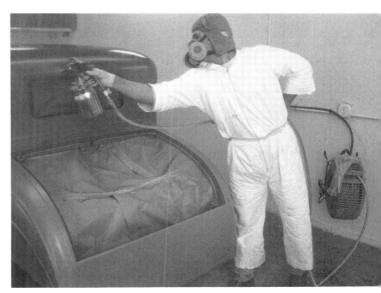

The first basecoat is a light 'tack coat." Because the basecoat is a metallic, it's very important to get even coverage. A total of four basecoats are applied, with a twenty minute wait between each coat (this is a PPG system, each paint product is a little different). Note how Jeff always keeps the hose away from the car.

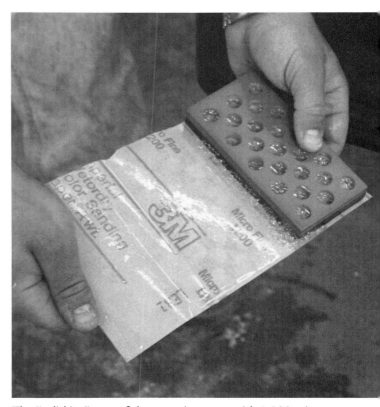

The "polishing" part of the operation starts with 1,200 grit, a sanding block and plenty of soapy water. This 1,200 grit paper will knock the tops off of the orange peel and flatten the surface for a great shine.

To avoid rubbing flat spots into the clearcoat, Jeff keeps the sanding pattern circular.

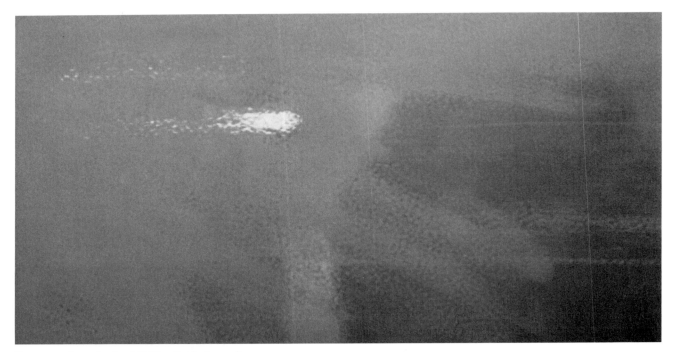

Part way through the 1,200 grit block sanding, you can see traces of orange peel in this close up shot. The idea is to flatten the surface until all the orange peel is eliminated.

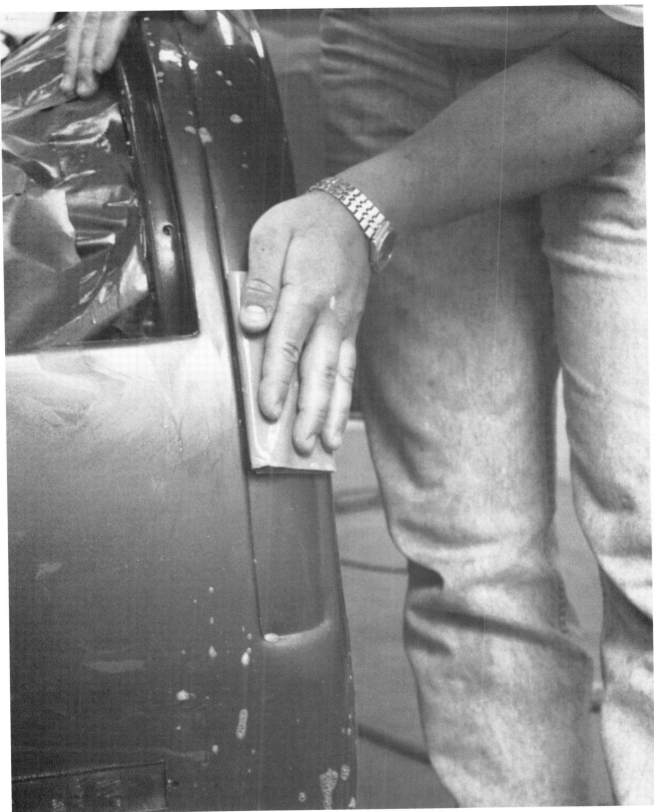

The next step is 1,500 grit paper and more block sanding with soapy water. With this step Jeff begins the process of eliminating sanding marks left by the 1,200 grit paper.

Though Jeff likes a stiff block for maximum flattening, a flexible pad must be used on curved areas like this one.

3M makes specific foam buffing pads for each of its polishing products. The foam pads help to eliminate swirl marks and are kept damp during operation, which keeps them cool as well.

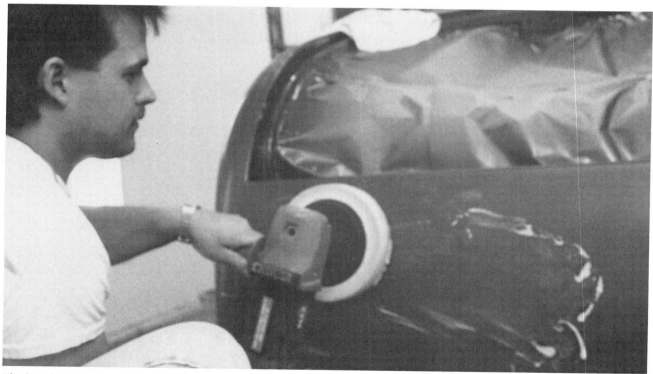

The liquid compound is applied to the car, then buffed with the electronic buffer. Buffer speed must be kept between 1,500 and 2,500 RPM, though it is better to err on the slow side of the recommendations. As always, Jeff is very, very careful with edges to avoid burning through.

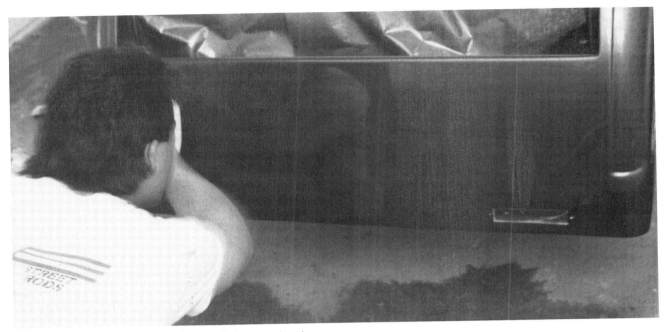

The final step is a glaze-type product applied by hand with a terry-cloth towel. When it's all over you should be able to use the panel as a mirror when you comb your hair.

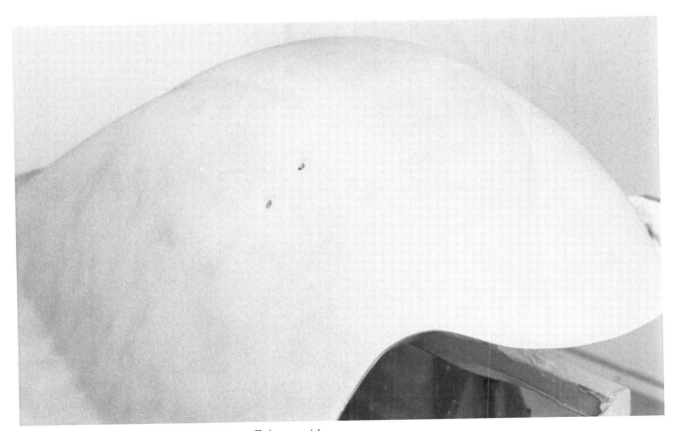

At this point, the 'glass fenders have been scuffed once with 240 grit, then sprayed with three coats of two-part primer surfacer and a light guide coat.

After test fitting the fenders to make sure they fit correctly, Jeff scuffs them with 240 grit paper. This will provide a surface that the next layer of material can stick to. While he's working the fenders with the sandpaper, Jeff is careful to knock down any little lumps in the gelcoat or imperfections at the edges of the fenders.

Following the sanding operation, the fenders are wiped down carefully with wax and grease remover and then with a tack rag.

Instead of spraying the fenders with primer, Jeff goes right to the primer-surfacer stage, explaining, "I can go right to a two-part primer surfacer like K-36 (known as

Because the fenders are in pretty nice shape, Jeff begins the block sanding with 400 grit and water, and won't have to do a second application of primer-surfacer.

Prima from PPG), and it will bond to the fiberglass just fine. And I'm not worried about corrosion between primer and the fender—so I just don't need that primer coat."

Jeff applies three coats of primer-surfacer, and allows the material to dry for 24 hours before he starts block sanding with 400 grit and plenty of water. Jeff starts off with 400 grit because the fenders are in such good shape to start with. Most metal fenders are going to need two applications of primer-surfacer and two separate block sanding operations.

In spite of the fact that the fenders are in good shape, the block sanding does show up a few low spots—and Jeff takes care of those with some two-part spot putty. In order to blend the spot-puttied areas with the surrounding area, Jeff uses 400 grit paper on a soft pad and a circular motion. In this way the fenders can be sealed and painted without the need for another application of primer-surfacer.

When the fenders are finished to Jeff's satisfaction, they are painted with basecoat and clearcoat, following the same sequence used on the rest of the car. In order

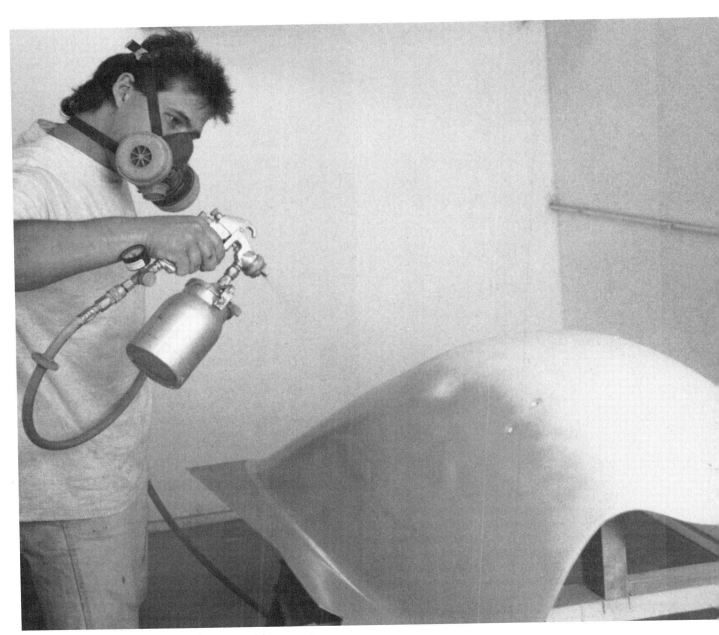

After block sanding and filling any low spots with spot putty, it's time for a sealer coat (DP 50 again) and then the basecoats.

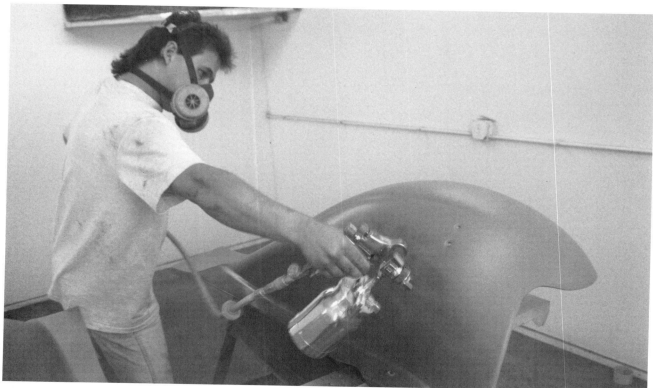

Jeff adds a product known as Stat-Free when he mixes the paint—in order to avoid troubles with static electricity that often crop up when painting fiberglass. The basecoat is laid on in four coats as it was on the body, being careful to achieve even application.

After application of the four coats of basecoat, the fenders are ready for the clearcoats and polishing, done in the same way and with the same steps as the body.

to avoid any trouble with static electricity, Jeff adds a product from Ditzler known as Stat Free to the paint. Otherwise the fenders are painted in the same sequence as the metal body.

The Finished Product

In the end, the Model A is rendered straight as a church picnic and carries a paint job with good color and good gloss. None of this happened by accident. Jeff's plan had many steps, and he carefully executed each one before moving on to the next. The materials Jeff used are all the most modern, and in each case he applied them as recommended by the manufacturer. It sounds preachy, but the difference between a great paint job and a mediocre paint job is in all the extra care that was taken throughout the job. It's all in the details.

Here are a few assembly pictures readers might find interesting. Note that the edge of the fender is covered with masking tape to avoid scratches while Jeff checks the final fit.

Once he's happy with the fit, Jeff leaves the fender loosely
mounted and pulls out the masking tape.

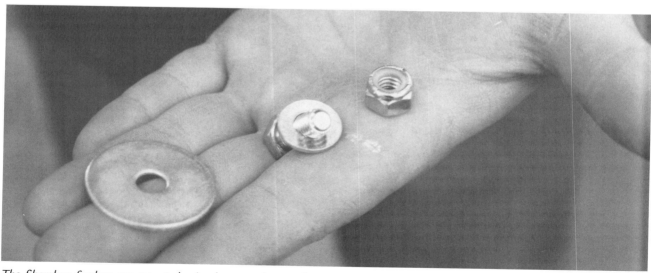

The fiberglass fenders are mounted using large washers and
Ny-Lock nuts—rather than conventional split lock washers.

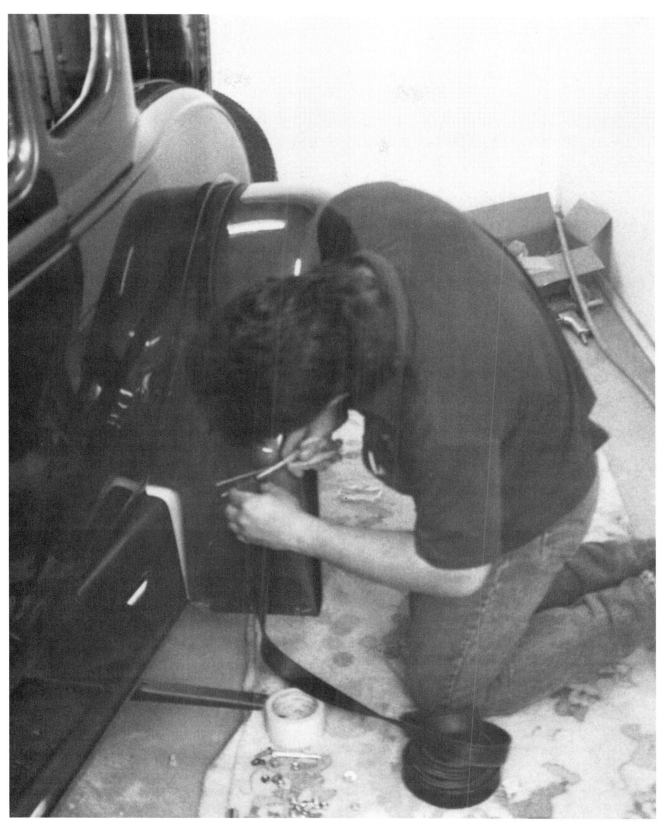

After the tape is pulled out, Jeff cuts the welting to fit and slides it in, between the fender and body.

*The "after" picture of a very nice Model A. One with straight
panels and great paint.*

Chapter 6

An Old-fashioned Paint Job Using Modern Materials

The paint job documented in this chapter was performed at Unique Body and Paint in Blaine, Minnesota. Most of the work was performed by Ron Gorrell, a man well versed in the art of creating flat smooth panels on hot rods and classics.

The car is a '48 Ford coupe; the paint job is essentially a color change on a car that's already built. While the color was being changed, some panels were further straightened, and some other mild bodywork was done, like the flush fit windshield and further finishing of the

The basic body work has been finished on this '48 Ford coupe, leaving the finish work and painting to be done. Before applying the first coat of primer-surfacer, Ron wipes the car down with wax and grease remover.

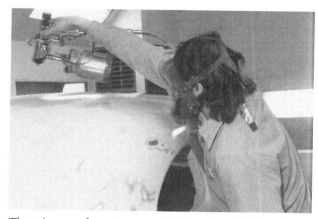

The primer-surfacer Ron uses is Prima from the PPG line, a two-part product that adheres well yet sands very easily. The primer-surfacer will be used to fill the scratches left from earlier work and to further flatten the panels. Here Ron applies the first coat of primer-surfacer to the roof. Note how he keeps the gun (an HVLP unit in this case) perpendicular to the surface.

bottom side of the car.

In the "old days" (note, however, that a number of people still paint this way) the true high-quality paint jobs were those where the painter applied multiple coats of lacquer to the car—with color sanding (or what is often called hand rubbing) between some of the coats. The idea then and the idea now is to apply a number of coats of paint, block sand the surface so it's perfectly flat, then apply another series of coats followed by more block sanding and polishing for a paint job with absolutely no wrinkles and a perfect gloss. Ron at Unique used this technique to paint the '48 Ford coupe. The only difference is that he used single-stage red urethane (designed to be used without a clearcoat) in place of lacquer.

The Preparation for Paint

When I came on the scene, Ron had already done nearly all the bodywork, and most of that bodywork had been block sanded with 80 grit paper. Where we begin to document the paint job is at the point where Ron starts

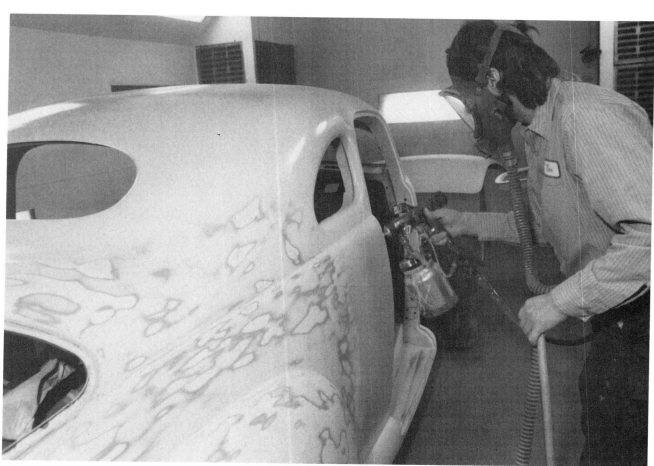

After spraying both sides of the roof, Ron moves down to spray the sides. Three wet coats of primer-surfacer will be applied, ten or fifteen minutes apart, so there is plenty of material on the car to fill low spots and sanding scratches.

the final prep before application of the finish paint—at the point where Ron sprays on the primer-surfacer and begins final block sanding.

Ron mixes up the two-part primer-surfacer (Prima or K-36 from PPG in this case) using the reducer of the correct temperature and the K 201 catalyst per the instructions (Ron prefers to work with the Prima mixed in standard form, not "high-build"). Ron applies three wet coats of this primer-surfacer, waiting a minimum of 10-15 minutes between coats. Areas like door edges where earlier sanding went through to the metal were treated first with metal prep before spraying the K-36. These first three coats of primer-surfacer are sprayed with the doors and trunk lid off the car. That way the jamb areas will also be coated with three coats of primer-surfacer and can then be finished to the same high degree as the body panels. After the three coats are applied, Ron allows the car to sit four or five days before beginning to block sand and adds, "If the weather's nice, I push the car outside and let it sit in the sun, because it is important that the material have a real good chance to dry and to release all the solvents."

Before he starts block sanding, Ron sprays the entire car with a darker guide coat of lacquer primer. As men-

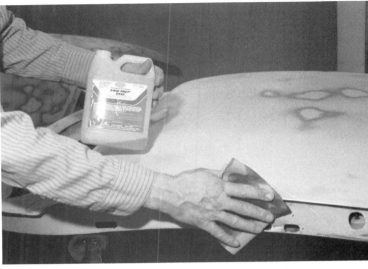

The doors are painted separately, but first any bare metal areas like the edges shown here are treated with one-step metal prep. Like the body, the doors get three wet coats of primer-surfacer. Ron likes to let the primer-surfacer dry for a few days before sanding so it has a chance to fully cure and shrink.

Before beginning the block sanding, the coupe is sprayed down with a guide coat to help highlight any low spots.

Ron and Steve re-mount the door, which will go on and off a number of times during the finishing process.

tioned before, a guide coat is a good means of finding low spots that might otherwise go unnoticed.

Ron and Steve Brunello remount the doors—a process that is made easier because the position of the hinges was marked before the doors were pulled off, that way they go back on the way they came off with only minimal adjustment. Though some painters sand directly across the door gap, Ron prefers to finish each edge separately and does minimal sanding across the door gaps.

Block sanding of the primer-surfacer begins with 120 grit paper. Flat surfaces like the doors are sanded with the idiot stick, sanding at 45deg to horizontal, and then at 90deg to the first sanding. This is sometimes referred to as "cross-hatching." Caution must be used with the idiot stick so grooves or flat spots are not sanded into the panels.

The more common curved panels found on this old coupe are sanded with a flexible sanding pad and 120 grit paper. This way Ron and Steve can get the panels smooth with a block that flexes to follow the curve of the

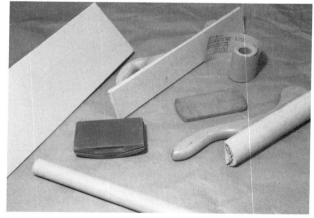

Different parts of the car call for different kinds of blocks for sanding. Here we see an oversized flexible block that works good on large round panels, and the common idiot stick (so long that even an idiot can get the panels flat), along with stiff and flexible smaller pads and rounded pads for special situations.

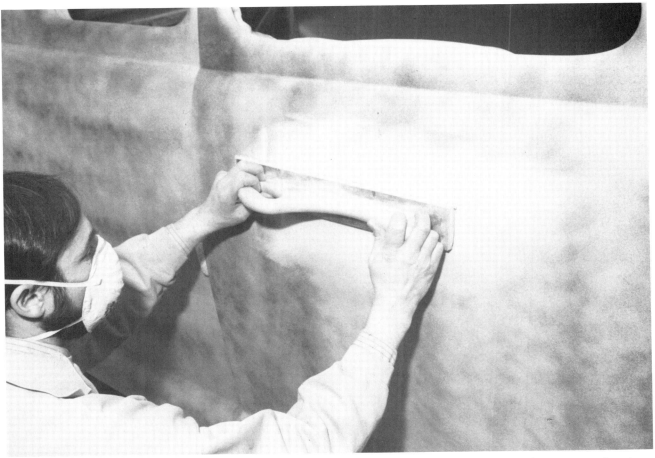

Ron sands the doors with the idiot stick equipped with 120 grit sand paper. In order to avoid sanding flat spots in the panel, Ron moves the sanding block in a diagonal pattern across the door. Here we see the sanding block moved down

and to Ron's left. After following this pattern a few times, Ron will change to a pattern that runs at 90deg and complete the "crisscross" sanding pattern.

panels. A paint stick is used to "slap" the paint dust out of the sandpaper and extend its life.

When the doors are sanded and Ron has checked the way the door skin matches the rest of the body panels, the doors are pulled off again, and the jamb areas are finished with a very flexible pad and more 120 grit paper. After the whole car is block sanded in 120 grit Ron fills a few low spots and pinholes with two-part spot putty.

After the first applications of K-36 are block sanded with 120 grit and low spots are filled, the car is sprayed again with three more coats of the same primer-surfacer. As before, Ron waits 10-15 minutes between coats, and then lets all three coats cure overnight (longer if possible). Before actually starting to sand the second application of primer-surfacer Ron and Steve (with a lot of help from their friends) mount the entire body to a large fixture like a rotisserie for a holiday turkey. In this way the bottom of the car can be finished to the same meticulous degree as the body panels on top.

Now the final block sanding can start. Sanding of the second application of primer surfacer is done with

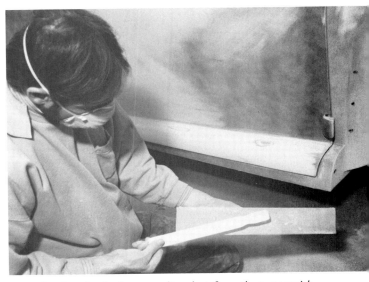

Ron often knocks the loose sanding dust from the paper with a paint stick to extend the life of each piece of paper.

101

360 grit paper and plenty of water. As before, a guide coat has been sprayed to help Ron identify any lingering low spots or pinholes. Though this final block sanding will further flatten the panels, the primary purpose of this step is to fill the 120 grit scratches left from the earlier steps. The primary tool used for this step is a flexible sanding pad—one that will easily follow the contours of this very round car—wrapped in 360 grit sanding paper.

As Ron works his way across the panels he is careful to keep the sandpaper wet with the sponge. He reminds readers that, "It's important to follow a crosshatch pattern so you don't sand flat spots into the primer-surfacer. Also, it's important to replace the paper often so it's al-

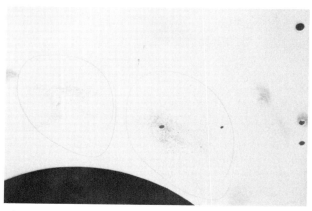

This close up shows two low spots left after the first round of block sanding. Low spots like this are filled with two-part spot putty, then block sanded to match the surrounding area.

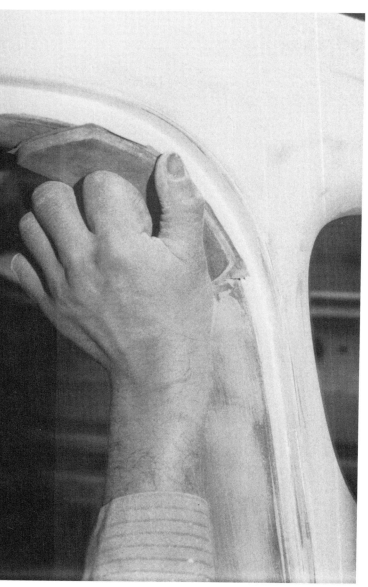

By applying the primer-surfacer with the door off, Ron was able to get plenty of material on the door jambs—so that later he could sand most of it off with this very flexible sanding pad.

ways nice and sharp, that way it will cut good and keep things flat. Dull paper will tend to follow small ripples and orange peel and won't cut or flatten the finish. You need lots of water to keep the paper clean and keep it cutting good."

After Ron sands an area, he inspects it to make sure it shows no guide coat, then he knows it's flat and ready for a sealer followed by the final topcoat.

Eventually the entire car is sanded in this way, flushed with water, wiped off with the squeegee and then inspected. As Ron finds no more low spots or pinholes in the filler or primer-surfacer, it's finally time for sealer.

Before Ron sprays the car with a coat of paint sealer, he goes over the vehicle with 3M Seam Sealer, a urethane caulk-type sealer. All the little seams in the floor or inside the gas filler opening that were not filled during earlier work are carefully filled with a neat bead of sealer. Ron smooths it with his finger and then further smooths it with a towel that's been dipped in reducer. Each of these sealer products is a little different so Ron is careful to follow the instructions. This 3M product is Ron's favorite because it can be painted over 10 minutes after application, and it won't shrink and crack later.

Paint It, Paint It, Paint It Again!

Ron is finally ready to spray the car with a single coat of sealer, but before doing that the booth is cleaned and the floor is watered down to trap any dust (remember that urethanes "like" extra humidity created by a wet floor more so than lacquers).

Ron uses DP 50 from PPG as the paint sealer, applied in one medium wet coat that will not be sanded. Like many paint products, this PPG material can be mixed in different ratios for different tasks. When the DP is mixed for use as a primer the ratio is 1:1, or one part DP epoxy primer and one part epoxy primer catalyst. When it is used as a sealer the recommended ratio becomes 1:1:1/2—or one part DP 50, one part epoxy primer catalyst, and one-half part the appropriate reducer (in this case DT 870) chosen for the temperature in the booth. The extra reduction helps the sealer go on nice and smooth; at this point Ron is not trying for a heavy film build.

As always, it's important to strain the materials as they go into the pot and measure each component carefully. Ron is careful to only mix as much as he is going to shoot that day, due to limited pot life of the epoxy materials.

Before the actual painting starts, Ron and Steve wipe the car down with wax and grease remover, then blow it off one last time, and finally wipe it down with a fresh tack rag. Ron goes so far as to blow himself off with compressed air before entering the booth to ensure that he does not take any dust inside with him.

Ron applies the DP 50 with a Mattson HVLP gun, set at 5lb cup pressure and 2 1/2lb air-cap pressure. Ron is very careful with the application, because this finish won't be sanded; it's important to put on a nice smooth layer of paint.

Ron starts on one side of the car and works up and over to the middle, then goes to the other side and works

The trunk lid is block sanded with the lid off the car, again using a flexible pad. As Ron sands through the guide coat the earlier body work shows through creating a pinto-pony effect.

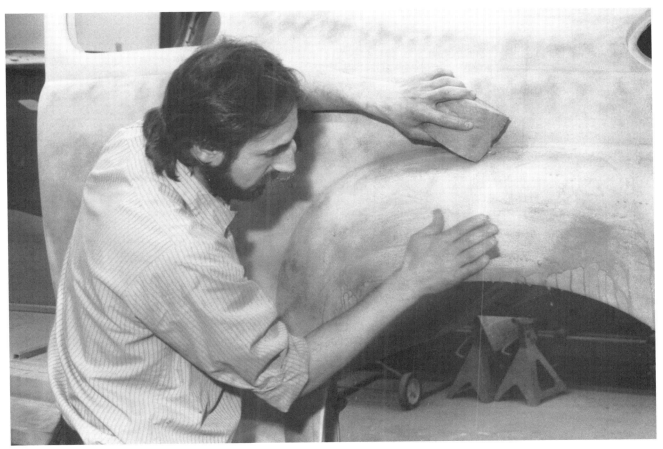

The coupe has received another three coats of primer-surfacer and a guide coat before being mounted to the rotisserie. Then Ron starts the block sanding again with 360 grit paper and soapy water.

After the final block sanding is finished and Ron is satisfied with the condition of the surface, Steve wipes the car off with wax and grease remover and then a tack rag before applying the sealer coat. 3M sealer is used for small seams and the Pre-Kleano is used as the wax and grease remover.

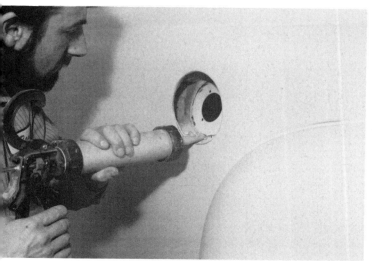

Here Ron uses the caulk-type sealer to seal the area inside the gas filler. This product can be painted over shortly after being applied.

from the middle to the side—this way there isn't a dry edge along the center of the car (as might happen if the painter started on the center, moved down to the side and then went over to the other side). After the DP 50 sealer coat has dried for 30 minutes (as always, there's a correct window of time before Ron applies the topcoat), Ron wipes the car off with a tack rag and gets ready for the first application of the red topcoat.

The entire car will be painted with Concept, an acrylic urethane from PPG that is usually a basecoat-clearcoat system, but is also available in a single-stage formula to be used alone without a clearcoat. As explained earlier, this car will be painted twice. After the car is painted once, it will be carefully color sanded. Then it will be painted and color sanded again. The idea is to apply a good film thickness, and then sand that surface ultra flat and paint the car again. Then it will be color sanded and polished one final time.

Now the red urethane is mixed using DU 5 as the catalyst, and DT 885 as the reducer. This DT 885 is a warmer reducer than would normally be called for, and

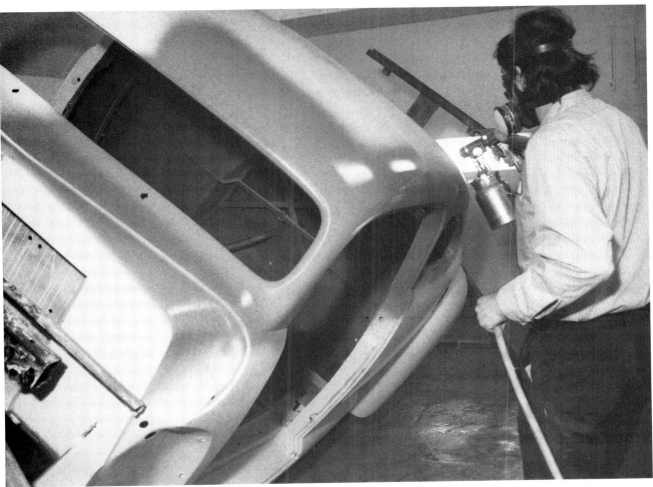

The sealer Ron uses is DP 50 from PPG, used to separate the final paint from the filler and also to achieve good color hold out. Note, when used as a sealer, this product is mixed with catalyst and the DT reducer of the correct temperature. Ron applies one coat of sealer to the car, working up to the center of the roof before...

Ron uses it because of the Mattson HVLP gun and because he's painting the whole car. Ron explains that, "With a regular gun I would use 870 but the 'warmer' reducer will help the paint flow better and seems to work better with the Mattson gun. I also use a warmer reducer (warmer reducers dry more slowly) when I paint a large surface or object, because the slower drying means that paint edges will melt together." As always, all materials are strained as they go into the pot, and recommended amounts and ratios are carefully followed.

Ron adjusts the Mattson gun to 6lb cup pressure and 3 1/2lb at the cap. Because this is a relatively heavy material Ron uses more cup pressure to help get the paint up to the cap and more air cap pressure to help break it up.

Note the sequence again—Ron starts painting on the driver's side at the side, works up to the middle of the roof, then they flip the car. For the other side, Ron starts at the middle of the roof and works to the side. He will apply three coats of the red, then it will be color sanded

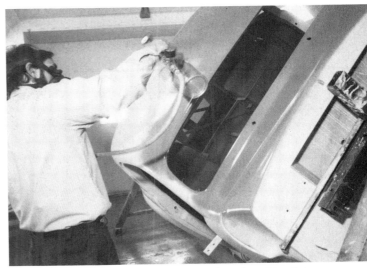

They rotate the car and begin painting the other side of the roof, starting from the center and moving to the side.

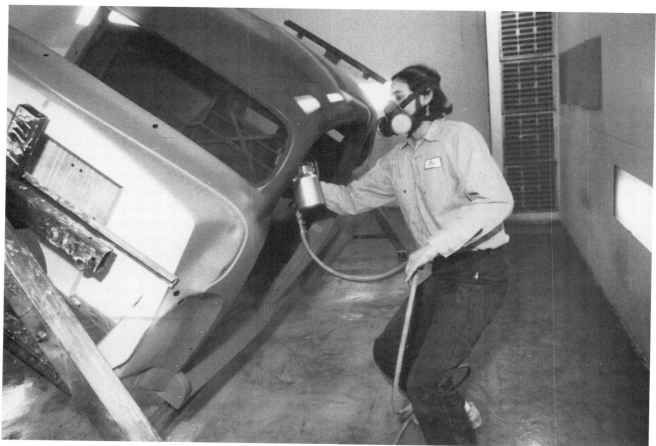

The finish paint for this project is Concept from PPG—a paint that's usually sprayed as a basecoat/clearcoat but will be used in single-stage form on this car. Ron applies the red Concept, starting from the driver's side of the roof. It's im-portant to get good coverage on the total car, including the door jambs. The car will get three coats of red during this "first application," all applied ten or fifteen minutes apart.

Ron always follows the same pattern, starting on the driver's side, then moving to the other side of the roof before moving on to the rest of the car.

before he puts on three more coats. He waits 10-15 minutes between coats, though he can't wait too long or the two coats might wrinkle. As always, painters *must* be careful to follow the recommended application times.

After the three coats of red have dried for two days (or longer, so the paint has ample time to dry), Ron and Steve start in with the color sanding. The idea is to flatten the surface and eliminate any orange peel before applying the final (the really final) topcoats. The color sanding is done with 500 grit paper that is kept wet, on a flexible sanding pad. It's important that the color sanding doesn't go through to the sealer or a light spot will result in the final paint finish. When Ron is satisfied that all the orange peel and any small imperfections in the paint have been eliminated, he wipes the car off again with wax and grease remover, tacks it with a fresh tack rag, and gets ready to apply three more coats of the urethane red.

The three coats of red are applied using the same procedure and dry times as was followed before. When the three final coats have dried for two days Ron and Steve are ready for the very thorough wet sanding and

After three coats of Concept, the coupe was color sanded with 500 grit paper and water. Then it was painted with three more coats of the red. Here is sits with six coats of red (re-member, a lot of paint has been sanded off) ready for more color sanding and then polishing.

polishing that will mark the end of this very thorough paint job. In a nutshell, the final sanding and polishing procedure starts with 600 grit wet and progresses through 1,200 to 2,000 grit before Ron and Steve go over the car with two different grades of polish.

Final Color Sanding and Polish

As before, the color sanding starts with a bucket of soapy water (the soap helps to lubricate the sandpaper), a flexible sanding pad, and plenty of 600 grit paper. Ron is extremely careful with the edges, going so far as to tape over the edges in the doorjambs. Other edges of body panels are treated with great care during the block sanding to avoid sanding through the paint.

After sanding quite thoroughly with 600, Ron uses a squeegee to dry the surface and then determine if it's time to start with the 1,200 grit.

Ron inspects the paint job for any imperfections, runs, orange peel, etc. The 600 is used to flatten the paint and eliminate all those imperfections. Ron looks

Before polishing, many of the most vulnerable edges are taped to avoid damage during the polishing operation.

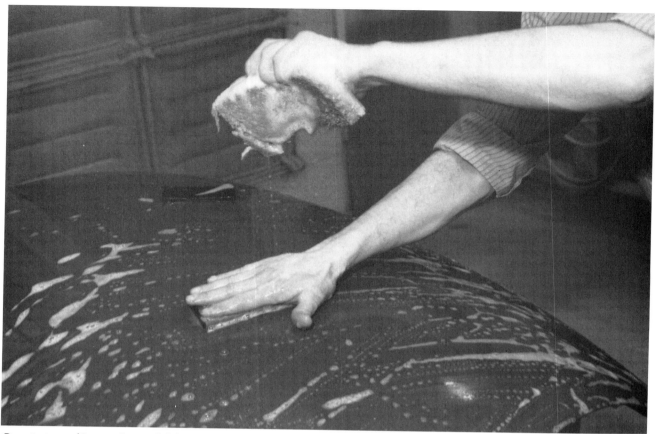

Ron starts working on the trunk lid with 600 grit paper on a flexible pad. A small squeegee makes quick work of drying the trunk lid before inspection. When he's finished with the 600 grit there should be no orange peel or imperfections—and then it's time for 1,200 grit.

The water is an important part of the color sanding—as it keeps the paper cool and flushes away paint debris.

for any areas or spots that are not uniformly flat, such as low spots and lingering orange peel. Some orange peel is discovered in the left lower corner of the trunk lid and what looks like a fish-eye in the lower panel, so he wets the trunk down and goes over the whole thing again.

Ron changes paper often, because "the fresh paper will help you to get the panel flat a lot faster." Because this is urethane, Ron starts with 600 and then progresses through two more stages of sandpaper before going to rubbing or polishing compound. With urethane paint Ron says that "the buffer will actually remove 1,200 grit scratches, but it's easier and less time consuming to go one more step and use some 2,000 grit first. That way the paint buffs easy, and you don't have to use a real aggressive compound. If the paint is lacquer, then I start with 600 grit then switch to compound and the buffer right away—without having to go through the other grits of sandpaper—because the paint is so much softer."

After he is satisfied with the flatness of the paint and the lack of imperfections it's time to start with 1,200 grit wet before progressing to 2,000 grit. Again, the flattening is done with the 600. The stages that follow will elimi-

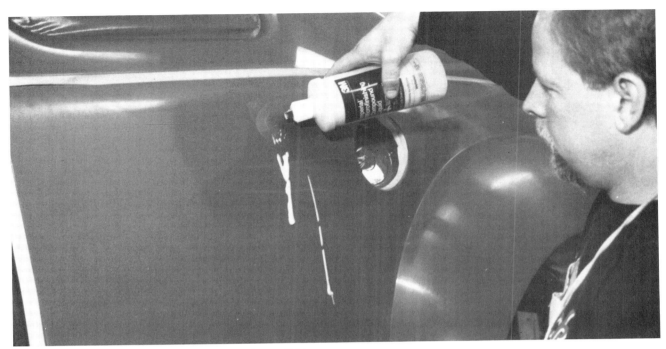

Here Steve applies the liquid compound (the first polishing step) to the body, rather than putting it on the buffing pad.

Ron and Steve use wool pads on the electric buffer to polish the body with the compound.

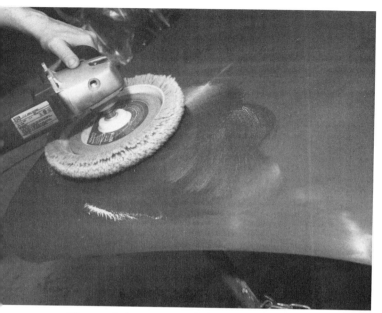

nate the scratches left from the 600 grit and provide a good shine. Ron says, "It's hard to know when you've gotten rid of all the 600 grit scratches, so I just go until I think I've got it good enough, and then I go a little further. And always remember you can only sand so much before you sand through, even on a flat panel. You need to know how much paint you've got on that panel."

When the entire car has been wet sanded with 2,000 grit, it's time to start on it with the buffer. There are numerous products available for buffing and polishing paint; Ron likes the materials manufactured by 3M.

For the initial buffing, Ron uses Imperial Microfinishing liquid compound #06011 from 3M in conjunction with an electric buffer. (Correct buffer speed ranges from 1750-2400rpm, though slower is generally considered better as there is less heat build up and less chance to burn through the paint.)

The liquid compound is put on the car, and then the buffer with a wool pad is used to spread it over a small area. Ron works one small area at a time and then applies more compound to the car and moves to another area. As Ron works over the paint with the compound, it begins to shine, though it leaves behind a definite haze. During the buffing, Ron advises first-time users to "always make sure the buffer is rotating so it's pulling itself

The trunk has progressed from 600 grit through 1,200 to 2,000 grit, and then to liquid compound. The last step for the buffer is the Perfect-it Foam Polishing Pad Glaze used with a special foam pad that helps eliminate swirl marks.

With the polishing almost finished and the body almost ready to go back on the chassis, the paint looks pretty good and shows some nice highlights.

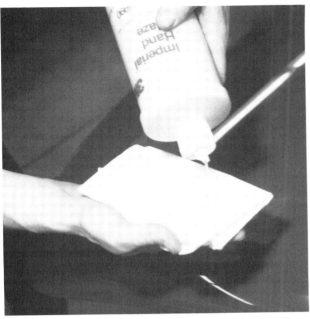

The last step is hand application of the Imperial Hand Glaze, done with a terry-cloth towel and plenty of elbow grease.

away from the panel. That way it will not 'catch' the edge and either damage the panel or burn the edge."

The final buffing is done with a special foam pad and some Perfect-It Foam Polishing Pad Glaze (both from 3M). This combination takes off the haze left from the compound and leaves the surface looking good. There is only one step left, the application of Imperial Hand Glaze from 3M. Terry-cloth towels are used for the hand application of the glaze. Ron puts some of the liquid on the towel, applies it in circular patterns to a small area and then lets it haze over before wiping it off like you would a good wax. This hand glaze will eliminate swirl marks, fill any tiny cracks in the paint, and leave the car with a great shine. All that's left is the final assembly—so the old Ford will become a car again.

In Review

Yes, it's an awful lot of work, more than twice the work of a reasonably good "normal" paint job. Ron went through two sequences with the primer-surfacer, followed by a paint job with color sanding, and, finally, another complete paint job with more color sanding and polishing. But the result is a very red coupe with very flat panels—and a truly remarkable shine.

The chassis has been finished, though not to the same degree as the body—only three coats of red and some selective polishing before being assembled with plenty of TLC.

Here it is—very red paint on very smooth, very flat panels showing a very nice shine.

Chapter 7

Pinstripes, Graphics and Flames

There's more to paint than just the application of a good Boyd Red or gloss black. Many painters like the idea of graphics, flames, or at least some pinstripes as a way to finish or add accent to a paint job. This chapter covers pinstriping, graphics, and flames—the one design that never goes out of style.

Pinstripes—Those Very Small, Very Important Stripes of Paint

A good paint job needs only a few accents to make it really "jump." A straight yellow might need blue or teal pinstripes to add a little contrast and a lot of accent. Pinstriping is one of those areas where you get a lot of im-

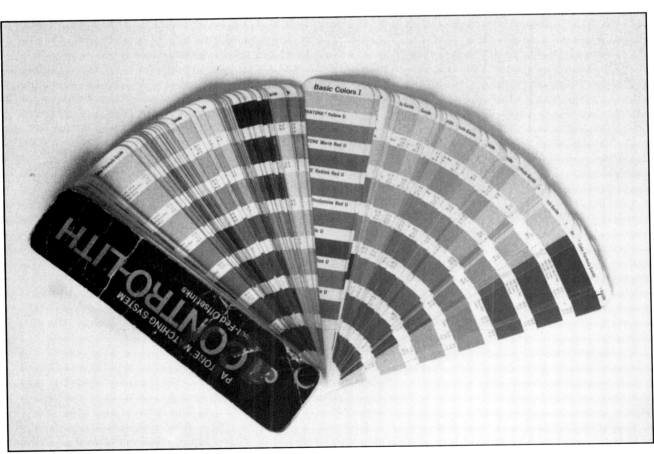

Some pinstripers use this PMS book to check how various color combinations work together. These books of color samples are available from most art supply houses.

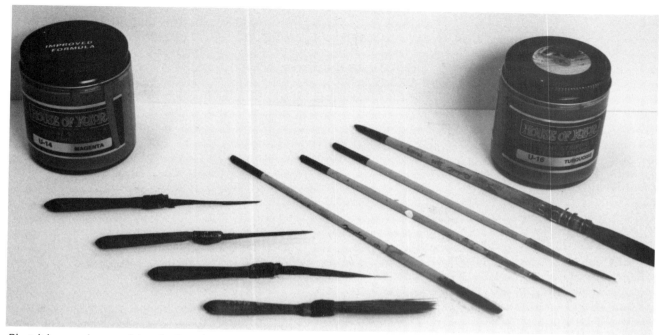

Pinstriping requires special tools. Seen here are the long bristled striping brushes on the left and some sign-painting brushes on the right.

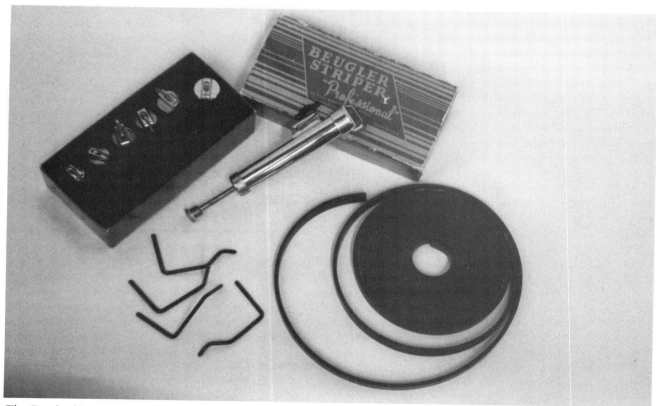

The Beugler kit, consisting of the body, a roll of magnetic tape, a selection of guide rods and a range of wheels for stripes of different widths.

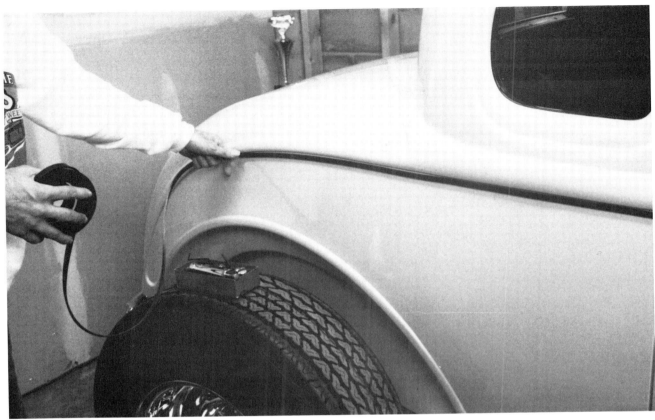

Here Eric Aurand runs the roll of magnetic tape across the
Deuce body before starting in with the Beugler.

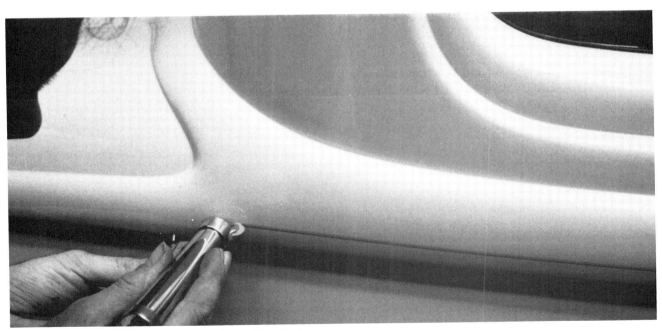

The Beugler is filled with paint and a guide rod is attached
(hard to see because it's on the bottom) and then the little
machine is pulled along toward the painter leaving a nice
straight line as it moves.

pact from a small amount of paint.

This pinstriping section covers the essentials of striping. Everything from tape to paint, from design to application. Whether you intend to pay someone else to stripe your rod, or to be really daring and do it yourself, there is information here that will make the task easier.

Many hot rodders, even those who insist on doing nearly everything themselves, shy away from the idea of doing their own pinstriping. Yet, there is no reason that a patient rodder can't do a simple pinstriping job at home.

Design

Choosing the colors and design for the stripes on your car requires experience and taste. If the car will be done by a professional pinstriper then the job is easy:

Just ask him or her for help and advice in the choice of the design and colors. If you're going to do the job yourself, it's a little more difficult.

Short of going back to school to study design, you should probably remember that less is more. This is an accent, not a complete paint job. You can always go back later and add another line or two. So pick a simple design, just one or two nice stripes that follow the natural lines of the car. Picking the right colors is more difficult. If you have an eye for color, then picking one or two colors to contrast and complement the main color might be an easy task. For the rest of us there are a few tools that make the job much easier.

Commercial printers use a PMS book as a color guide. Available from a graphic art supply house, the PMS book contains hundreds of color samples and the

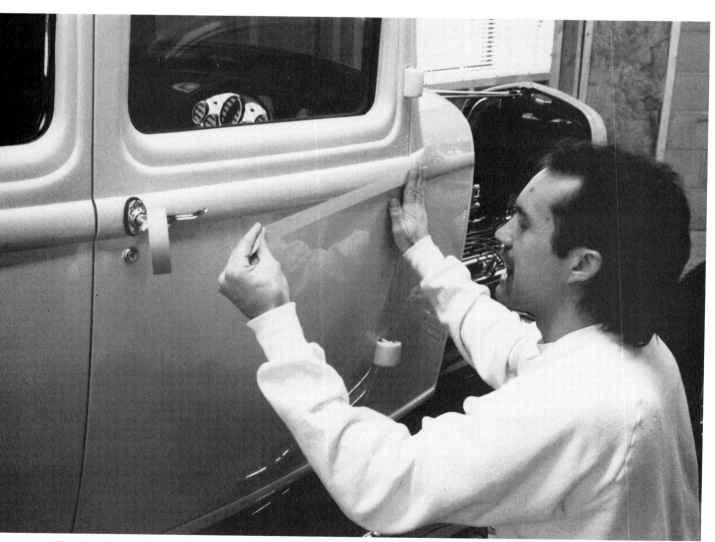

Fine Line Striping Tape is like a series of thin rolls of masking tape all on one roll. 3M makes this tape in two different configurations, each with a different number of "pull outs." Before putting on the tape—or doing any kind of striping for

that matter—it's important to clean the body with a Prep Sol type cleaner. Here Eric puts the tape down nice and straight. It's important that the tape be well stuck to the car so paint won't migrate under the edge.

116

A single "pull out" is removed prior to laying down the first stripe.

After choosing a good color, Eric pulls the first line. The brush should always be pulled toward the painter. Next, Eric will pull another pull out and then lay down a different color.

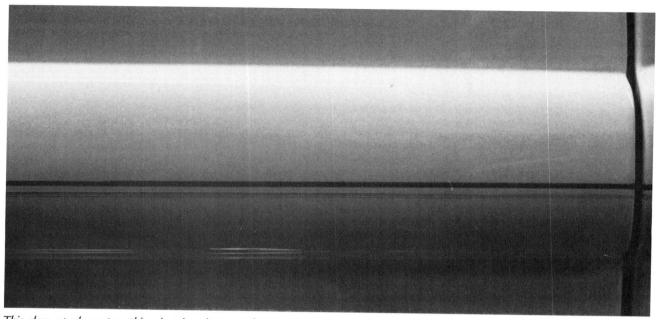

This close up shows two thin pinstripes in two colors on the Deuce after the tape has been pulled. Looks nice and neat to me.

Brian Truesdell from St. Paul, Minnesota wouldn't be caught dead using that old Fine Line Tape. Brain does his work free hand, though as we see here, he does sometimes use a little masking tape as a guide.

formulas for making them. Find a color you like and hold it up next to the door or quarter panel to see how the two colors look together. Though the book and the formulas are intended for a commercial printer, you will at least get an idea how much of each basic color a particular shade contains. Another good source of color ideas is the paint chip cards available from various paint manufacturers. Though there aren't as many shades as a PMS book, the color cards are still a good way to try various combinations to see how they work together.

As a final note, many stripers feel that two stripes in two different colors have much more visual impact than a single line or two lines in one color. The two colors, if carefully chosen, work off each other as well as off the color of the car to create more impact.

Tools of the Trade

Pinstriping requires special tools and materials. At the top of the list are the brushes, those funny looking brushes with the short handles and the extra-long bristles. On a good brush those long bristles are usually camel or squirrel hair (most professionals don't like synthetic brushes). The brushes are rated numerically, from 0000 to 5, with 0000 being the smallest (and 0000 can be hard to find) and 5 the biggest. Though the professional might have ten or more brushes in use, the beginner only needs half that many to get started. Three or four brushes from a company like Mack or Dagger are probably enough to get you started.

Each pinstriper seems to have his or her own formula for cleaning and maintaining their brushes. Brian Truesdell, a well-known striper from St. Paul, Minnesota,

Note that Brian takes the sign painting enamel off the white card—that way he can feel the thickness of the paint and better control the shape of the brush. The key to good pinstriping is learning to properly thin the paint.

119

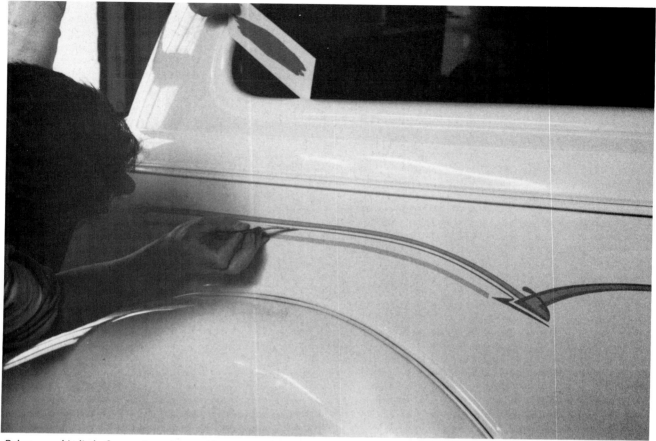

Brian runs his little finger along the masking tape as he pulls a nice line along the side of this old Chevrolet. The card in his left hand holds the paint.

Lenny starts the job of putting graphics and stripes on Scott's Model A with a sketch showing the basic design and the colors. The first job is always cleaning, so the paint will stick and won't react with dirt or impurities on the car.

likes to clean them with mineral spirits (he also uses mineral spirits to thin his One-Shot and Chromatic paints). Brian keeps two cans of mineral spirits on the bench, using the first one to clean most of the paint from the brush and a second can of cleaner spirits for the final cleaning. After cleaning the brushes Brian wets them down with clean engine oil and lays them out flat until they are used again.

Masking tape has a variety of uses in the pinstriping process. Professionals like Brian often use a single piece of 1/4in masking tape as a guide to follow as they move the brush along the side of the car. Good free-hand pinstriping requires years of experience and is probably a no-no for the novice. Instead, 3M manufactures a unique tape product—actually many thin pieces of tape on one roll—that makes the job much simpler (more on this tape later). The most important thing to remember about masking tape is to always buy a brand name from an auto parts store. All masking tape is not created equal. Some is meant for home use and some just isn't very good. Use the cheap tape from the discount store and you risk tearing off the original paint when you pull off the tape.

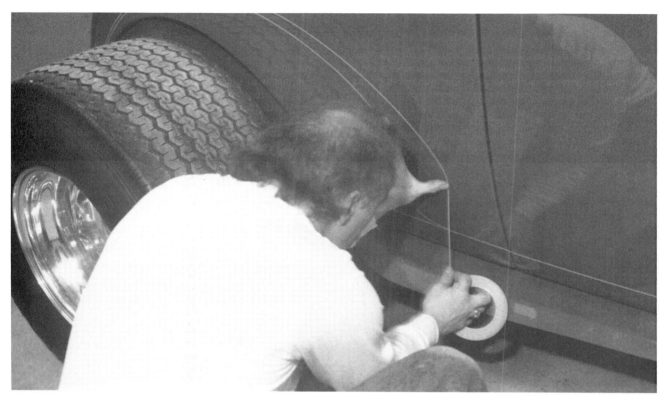

Lenny lays out his design free-hand with thin, Fine Line tape from 3M. Note how the two hands work together to correctly position the tape.

After one side is done to his satisfaction, Lenny takes a few measurements and lays out the other side. Remember, no one can see both sides at the same time.

The paint used for pinstriping is usually a special paint known as sign painting enamel. This paint is special in that it is designed to be inert. Sign painter's enamel can be laid down over the car's paint without any fear that the two paints will react, no matter what type or brand of paint is on the car.

Probably the best known striping paint is One-Shot Sign Painting Enamel. Another paint choice is Chromatic Lettering Enamel. Designed again as an inert paint, the Chromatic is available in a large range of colors, all designed to be applied over other paints.

Perhaps the brightest and most durable of the striping paints is a product offered by Jon Kosmoski's House of Kolor. Jon's Sign and Lettering Enamel is the only true urethane striping paint and offers the durability that only a urethane can achieve. In addition, the House of Kolor paints offer a wide range of wonderfully bright colors. These striping paints can be used as a straight one-coat urethane (with a catalyst in the paint) or they can be used un-catalyzed and clearcoated after application. If the urethane is clearcoated the catalyst is added to the clearcoat.

Special Tools for Striping at Home

Novice pinstripers can't be expected to pull a straight line like the professionals. For amateur pinstripers there are a couple of tools and techniques that make the job much easier.

One of these is the Beugler, a pinstriping machine that comes complete with all the accessories you might

After laying out the design, Lenny finishes the taping with wider masking tape.

Dark gray is the first color to be painted on the side of the car. Lenny works fast so the gray will still be wet when the black is applied next.

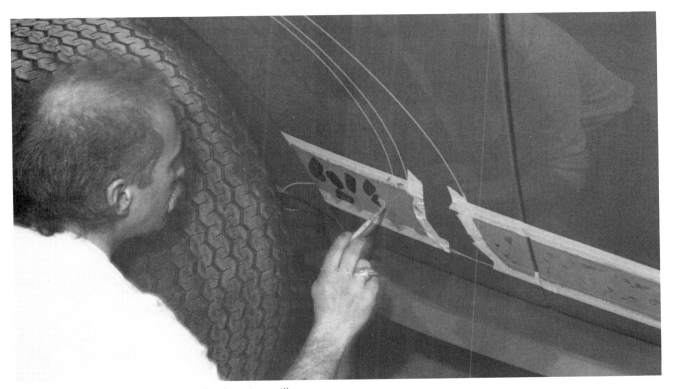

The black is dabbed on next with another lettering quill.

need. Think of it as a small wheel, constantly supplied with fresh paint—a paint-wheel that you roll along the side of your car. With a little practice, the line you leave behind will be consistent and straight, done without the bother of applying masking tape.

The Beugler actually comes as a kit, consisting of the basic body (or paint reservoir), a series of "wheel-heads" and an assortment of guide rods. The wheel-head contains the little wheel that runs along the side of the car. Each head has a wheel of a different width—the wider the wheel, the wider the line (pretty complicated science here), all the way from ultra thin to fat and hairy.

To get started you pull off the head, pull back the plunger, and fill the body with paint. Though you need to thin the paint you apply with a brush, the Beugler works best when filled with paint straight from the can. Next, put on the head with the appropriate wheel to create a line as wide as you desire. Before heading directly to the car, there is one more important step. Creating a straight line means following a guide. Provided with the Beugler kit is a roll of magnetic tape. Before starting across the car with the Beugler full of paint you must lay the magnetic tape across the body. This is your guide, so lay it across the car, bend it to follow the body lines, and then stand back and make sure it runs straight and smooth. Mount one of the guide rods in the Beugler and let the guide rod run along the edge of the magnetic tape as you pull the Beugler along toward you.

The magnetic tape obviously doesn't work so well in the case of fiberglass bodies or steel bodies with a lot of bondo under the paint. In order to avoid scratching the paint you will have to be sure the tape is wiped clean before you stick it to the car.

Depending on the design and placement of the stripes on your car, the reveal lines might be used in place of the magnetic tape. In this case, you need to

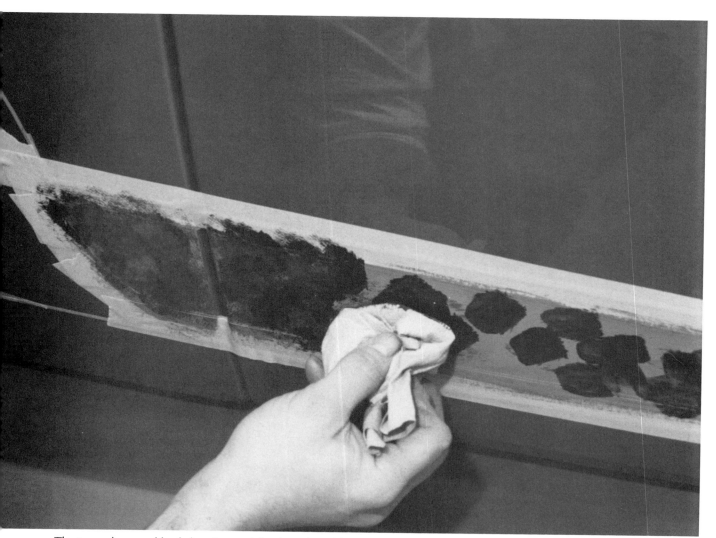

The two colors are blended as Lenny dabs the paint with a rag (a small sponge works better).

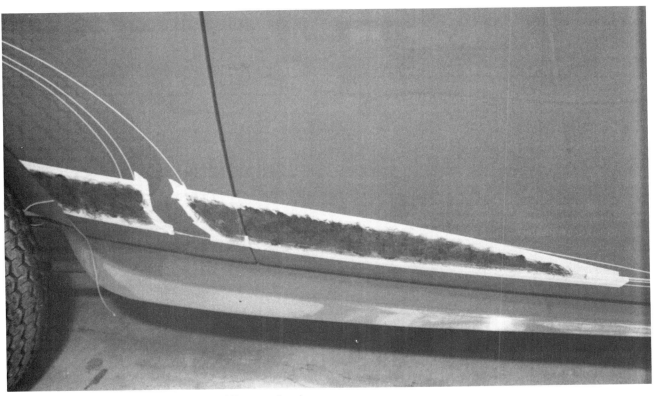

Here's the side with the first step of the marbling completed.

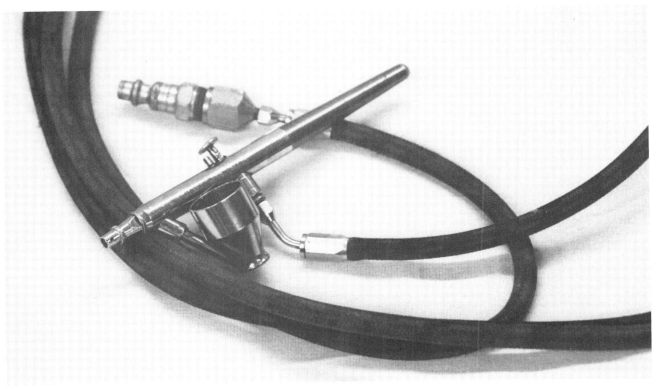

Lenny's air brush is just a mini spray gun with a two-stage trigger, designed to run on 20psi.

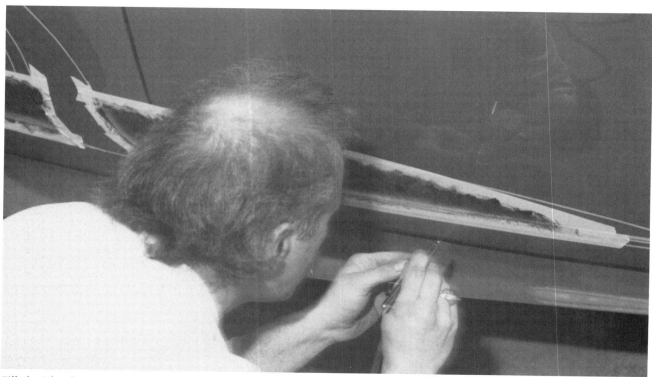

Filled with white paint, the air brush is used to create a lighter area along the bottom of the marbled section and lighter stripes running diagonally across the dark areas. The paint in the air brush is chromatic striping and lettering enamel thinned slightly so it will pass through the gun.

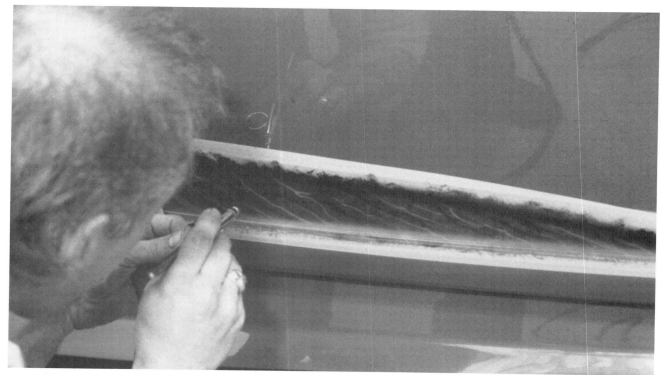

More delicate air brush work is used to paint a dark band along the top and dark diagonal stripes.

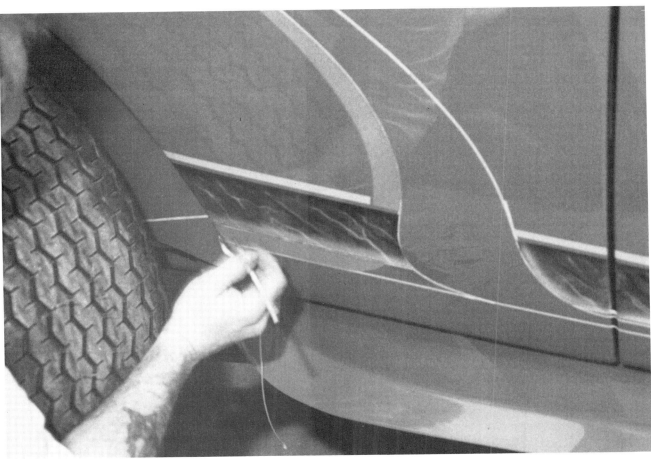

Next comes a gray stripe along the top of the marbled section done with a short-bristle lettering quill. Then it's time for the smaller stripe arching over the wheel shown here, with a

matching stripe ahead of the rear wheel—both are done with a lettering quill.

choose a guide rod that puts the Beugler the correct distance away from the reveal, and then just pull the Beugler toward you as you would using the magnetic tape as the guide. Reposition the guide rod and you can go back and add a second line in a second color, parallel to the first.

Like any other tool, the Beugler works best when it's kept clean. After each use you need to strip the whole thing down to the bare body and immerse it in the thinner of your choice. Failure to clean it thoroughly will result in a plunger that is stuck permanently in the body.

First-time pinstripers have another tool that makes the job of pinstriping much easier. This product is a special masking tape called 3M Fine Line Striping Tape.

Think of it as six or eight thin strips of masking tape on one roll. You put the wide masking tape on straight and smooth, and then you pull out one of the small strips to leave an opening ready for paint with masking tape on either side of it. If you need a heavier line, just pull two of the "pull-outs." This is a good product for the home-striper. In fact, some of the professional stripers use this tape in tough situations.

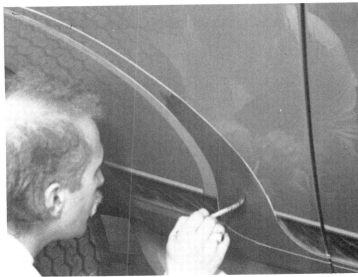

Finally, it's time for the large arch over the rear wheel, done with a lettering quill that's too big for the small areas and two small for the big areas.

This is the finished product, a marbled multi-dimensional graphic along the sides of the car.

In contrast to the very modern graphic, Lenny and Scott decide to add some very traditional pinstripes to the front and rear of the coupe. Lenny paints—the same three colors used for the graphics will be used for the stripes—from a small Dixie cup. Lenny starts slow, working free hand from the center out. Stripe by stripe, the design grows across the trunk lid.

If the magic tape has a downside, it is the tape's inability to flex. Anything more than a mild curve will have to be done freehand, or with two pieces of 3M plastic tape laid out side by side, the width of one pinstripe apart.

If the design is simple and nearly straight you can just put on the tape, pull out one strip and apply the paint. The key to success is in making sure the car is clean, making sure the tape goes on straight and making sure that it sticks. Once the tape is applied, pull one "pullout," and use your new brush to pull a nice line. It's a good idea to push down both edges of the tape as you move along. The second "pullout" can be removed after the first color is applied. Now just put on the second color and pull off the tape.

Just Do It!

Laying down a nice line is a special skill acquired after considerable practice. Brian Truesdell, a pinstriper since 1974, suggests that beginners use 3M tape or a special tool like the Beugler until they have considerable experience. He also stresses the important role that preparation pays in a good striping job.

Before applying the tape or trying to lay down a line, the surface must be clean, very clean. Prepsol, a cleaning solvent, is commonly used by professional stripers (after a very thorough wash job) to remove any old wax or any film on the paint. Special sign painters' Prepsol is available for problem areas. One of the biggest headaches for a striper is removing waxes and polish that contain silicones. Some people apply a little of the striping paint on a small area of the body before the actual striping begins. If the new paint "fish-eyes," then more cleaning is needed. In a worst case situation, fish-eye eliminator can be added to the striping paint (though it does weaken the striping paint).

Once the surface is ultra clean, the striping can begin. If you use the 3M tape you have the option of one or two lines of various sizes. The design will depend on the style you've chosen for the car and your personal taste. When in doubt, remember that less is more (thin lines generally look more professional than fat ones). Besides,

you can add to the striping later. With the multiple pull-outs of the 3M tape, you can easily run two parallel lines of different colors along the contours of the quarter panel and doors.

Laying down a nice, consistent line is in large part dependent on learning how to correctly thin the paint. You need the right consistency so the brush puts on a nice even line. Thin the paint too much and the line spreads and has no definition. Thin it too little and the line is dry with bare spots where no paint was transferred from the brush to the panel or door. As a starting point, Brian suggests you try one part paint to one-quarter part thinner. Always pull the brush toward you; never move it across or away from you.

Brian Truesdell uses the small, 3 ounce (oz) Dixie cups for the paint mixing (larger cups have a wax coating that mixes with and contaminates the paint in the

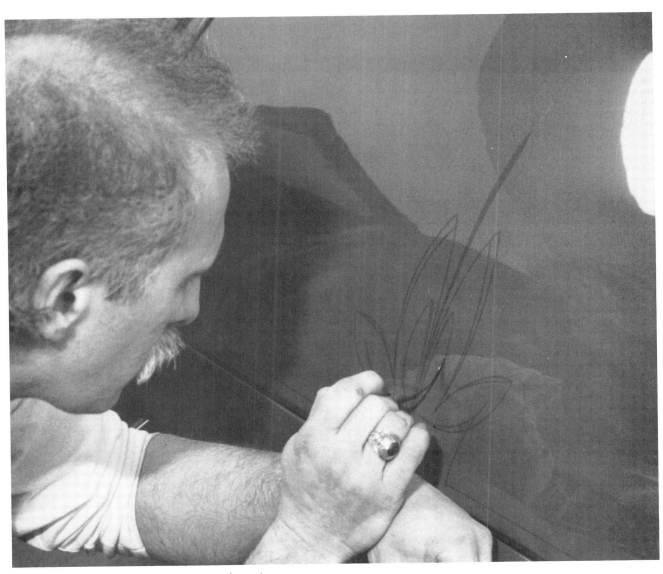

The symmetrical design becomes more complex as it grows.

After a lot of work, done in three colors, Scott is left with this lovely design on the trunk lid.

cup). Once you think you've got the paint mixed to the correct consistency, brush some on a small white card and "feel" how thick the paint is and how the brush drags as it moves across the card. Brian takes his paint from the card, instead of from the little cup. Dragging the brush across the card allows him to check the thickness of the paint and also helps to keep the brush in its correct shape. If the paint refuses to flow correctly a little linseed oil can be added as a thinner. This has no effect on the paint itself other than to slow the drying time slightly.

You're probably thinking, "What if I make a mistake?" Mistakes, at least fresh ones, can be wiped off with a rag. Even the next day, One-Shot or Chromatic enamel can usually be taken off with thinner and a clean rag. When using the urethanes you have to be more careful, as they adhere with more tenacity to the surface underneath.

Brian offered the following list of "helpful hints" for the first-time pinstriper:

The radiator shell gets a similar, though not identical design. The colors used in the pinstripe are the same colors used in the graphics.

The final shot, a very nice Model A coupe set off with just enough pinstriping and graphics.

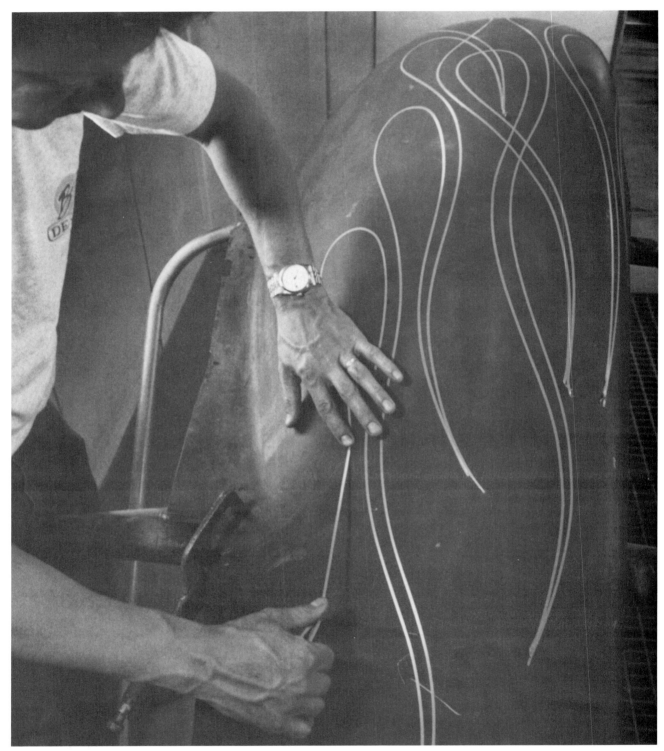

This is the start of a "demo" project—painting tri-color flames on an old Deuce fender. Here, Brian Truesdell, of St. Paul, Minnesota, lays out the pattern free-hand, using 1/8in-thick blue fine line tape from 3-M. Brian likes the plastic tape because it turns without breaking, making it easier to lay out a complex pattern. Brian works by eye, and doesn't start with any pattern drawn out on the fender. He controls the tape by pulling it with one hand while guiding it with the oth- er. If he doesn't like the way a flame lick lays down, he just pulls up the tape and starts over. Brian always uses two hands, one to put tension on the tape and the other to guide it. Before starting, Brian is careful to clean his hands, and also tries to minimize how much he handles the fender during the layout to minimize the transfer of oil form his hands to the fender.

Back-taping is done with a good grade of 3/4in masking tape. Brian tries to put down the masking tape so there is always some of the blue fine line tape showing through at the edge—and recommends against putting the tape down in a sloppy fashion and cleaning it the edges up later with a razor blade. Still, places where the flames overlap and the ends of some flame licks must be cut out with a razor blade. With the taping almost finished, you can actually see the shape and design of the flames. This is the time to critique the flames. If you don't like the shape or pattern, don't be afraid to pull the tape and start over.

· Anytime the stripes are laid down over a fresh paint job, one only a few hours old for example, the striping paint tends to stick better and quicker to the paint underneath, leaving less time to wipe off mistakes. When pinstripes are to be laid down over a fresh urethane paint job, the urethane should dry for two or three days first. Otherwise the tape applied over the fresh paint job may cause the urethane to wrinkle.

· If you choose to do it yourself with the help of the 3M tape, it's critical to make sure the tape sticks correctly. Run your thumb or forefinger along the tape just before applying the paint to ensure that the edges are really stuck down.

· With plastic or fiberglass surfaces static electricity can be a problem. The simple cure is to wipe the surface down with a damp rag prior to painting.

· The key to a good striping job is in choosing good color combinations, keeping your design simple, and taking your time. This is definitely a case where haste makes waste.

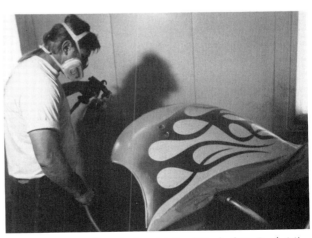

Before he starts the painting, Mallard Teal of St. Paul, Minnesota, wipes the fender off with a tack rag. Because of all the tape, you really can't wipe the fender down with wax and grease remover. Mallard starts the painting part of the project with a light primer coat to ensure good adhesion.

These three-color flames will start in yellow, fade to orange, and then go to red. All the paints are straight one-step colors, not candy colors. Mallard likes to start at the darkest end and work toward the lighter end. The gun is a conventional high-pressure gun running at 40psi.

Don't Forget ...

Pinstriping is a case where a few details make a lot of difference. With a few helpful tools and a little practice on that old hood behind the garage, there is no reason you can't do the pinstriping yourself.

Hands On: Lenny Does a Modern Graphics and Stripe Job

The car seen here is a Model A coupe belonging to Scott Winger of Cambridge, Minnesota. Scott is owner of Scott's Auto Body in Cambridge. The pinstripe artist is Lenny Schwartz of Krazy Kolors Signs in St. Paul, Minnesota.

This job is an especially good one to document, as it is a combination of modern graphics and traditional pinstriping—and uses at least three different tools and techniques to get the job done. The design is a collaboration between Lenny, Scott, and Scott's wife, Joan. To make sure they all see the same design, Lenny starts with a simple sketch of what the graphics on the side of the car will look like, and they all agree on the design and the colors.

The first step is to wipe the car down with Prepsol so the new paint will stick. Lenny advises that if the car is very dirty, it should get a good washing first. Next, Lenny starts the taping on the car, using thin, Fine Line tape from 3M. Lenny uses the sketch as a guide, then lays the tape out free-hand on the sides of the car. If he doesn't like the way the tape lays out, he just pulls it and starts over again. After Lenny is happy with the design on one

side, he takes a few key measurements, and then transfers the design to the other side.

During this layout work, Lenny is careful to keep his fingers off the car as much as possible, so no oils are transferred from his hands to the paint.

After the Fine Line tape is applied on both sides, Lenny finishes the taping job with wider tape. The paint he uses in the airbrush is Chromatic Striping and Lettering Enamel. Lenny will do a marbled section first, working with a #12 lettering quill. Lenny starts dark and goes light, though you can go either way depending on your personal style.

Lenny starts with dark gray paint, applied with the brush. With marbling you have to be careful how quickly it dries, because you want to come back and "sponge" the finish while it's still in liquid state, so you get a mix of the two colors. Next, Lenny dabs on some splotches of black and then pats them with a bunched up rag—though a sponge works better for this than a rag.

The next step calls for the airbrush. Lenny loads it with Chromatic paint again, thinned out so it will pass through the airbrush, and uses the airbrush to create a 3-

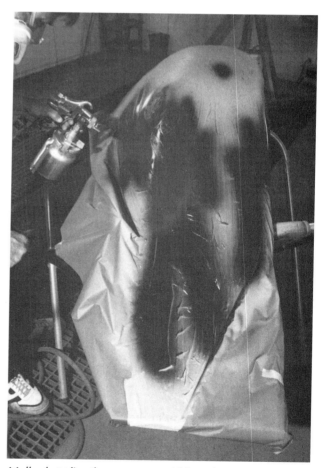

Mallard applies the orange, or middle, color next. He doesn't worry too much about blending the colors at this point and will go back and touch up the blended areas later.

D effect and some detail to the marbling. He starts by adding a lighter line along the bottom of the marbling, and some "cracks" across the surface. Then a dark band is added across the top for a 3-D effect and also between the light streaks that run at a diagonal to the stripes. There is some overspray here, which Lenny wipes off with thinner on a rag (or you could just do a more thorough job of masking the panels). Next, Lenny adds the gray stripe along the top of the marbling. This is done with a #6 lettering Quill.

He mixes up a purplish-blue, a combination of process purple and brilliant blue. He mixes it until he likes the color, then adds a little bit of white to lighten the color slightly. Lenny suggests that, "It's a good idea to do a little test area to see how the colors work with the overall color and the other graphic colors, so you don't make any mistakes and get a color that just doesn't work. If you don't like the color, it can always be wiped off."

For the big stripe that arches over the rear wheel, Lenny uses a #10 lettering quill. This is a compromise size, or a brush that is too big for the small areas and too small for the big areas.

For the final effect, Lenny does some fine free-hand pinstriping on the nose and the trunk lid, with a very fine

The last color to be applied is the yellow, or lightest color. Using a regular gun, Mallard next goes in and touches up the tips of flames that got too orange during earlier spraying. He will later use orange paint in a touch up gun to darken the front edges of the flames, and the last steps are to touch up the blended areas where two colors meet.

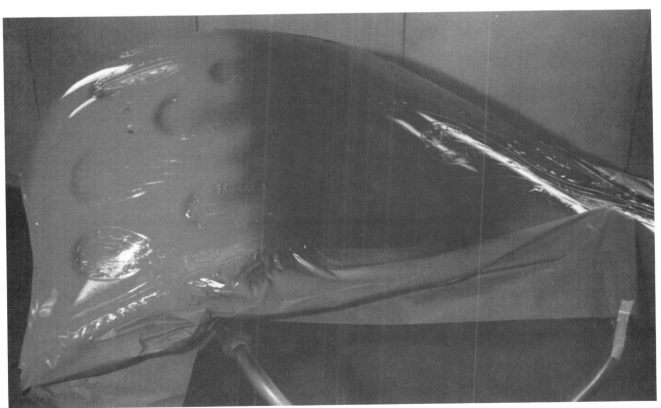

This is the finished fender before the tape is pulled. Mallard says the way to paint flames like these successfully is: 1. Get the three main colors down, don't worry about the blends. 2. Then go back into the areas where the two colors meet and do the blending. 3: To blend solid colors, reduce the paint 200 percent, turn down both the air to the horns and the material control knob (and air to the gun). Then go back and blend the areas where the two colors meet with the lighter of the two colors using your eye as a guide.

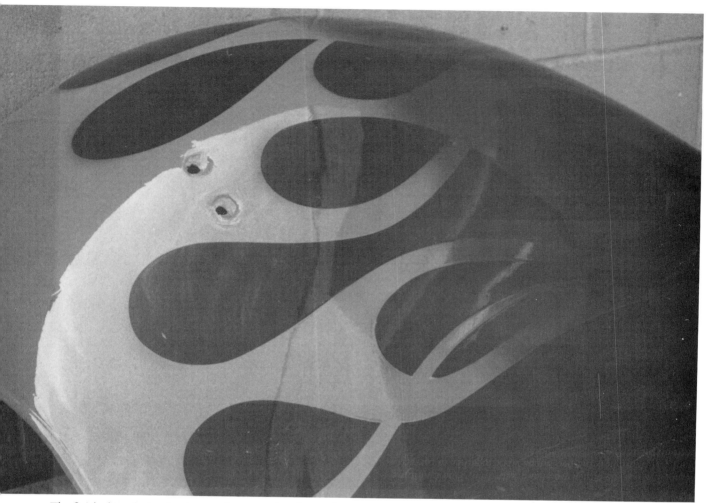

The finished product, after he tape is removed and everything is covered in a clearcoat. Pinstripes can be used to brighten the flames if needed, and also to clean up any rough paint edges where the flames meet the surrounding paint. Remember, the three keys to a good flame job are: Start with a good shape, pick good colors, and do nice blends.

brush, a size 00 cut in half (to make his own 0000). He uses the same colors for the pinstripes as he did for the graphics so that everything will work together. Lenny stops long enough to explain that with pinstriping, it's very important to learn to thin the paint correctly. Some people like Brian work off a card so they can feel the paint. Lenny works off the edge of the Dixie cup (note, the small Dixie cups work better because they have no wax coating). He does one color on one end, goes to the other end with the same color, then changes colors. In total he uses three colors on the coupe.

Chapter 8

Painting the Frame

Whether the frame you're working on is a new reproduction unit from Pete and Jake's or Chassis Engineering, or one of Henry's originals, it no doubt needs a little help in the appearance department. Some rodders insist that their frame be finished to the same high degree as the body, with all the welds filled and the paint rubbed out by hand. Others will settle for a simple paint job done either in black or in a color to match the rest of the car.

This chapter covers most of the situations you're likely to encounter. Paint and filler materials, preparation

This is the "before" picture of the '41 Ford frame at Pete and Jake's facility in Kansas City, Missouri. The stock frame has been sandblasted to remove most of the rust.

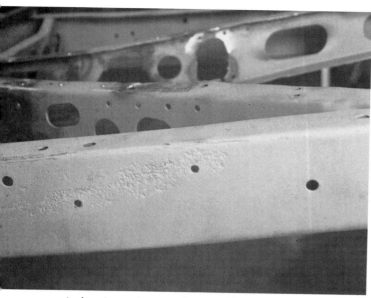

techniques, and application of paint are all here. The Hands On section documents the preparation and painting of an original Ford frame at the Pete and Jake's shop. If it's an engine you're trying to paint, then move to the back of the chapter. There you will find a similar discussion of preparation techniques and the best materials for the job. Another Hands On section follows the painting of an engine at the Twin Town shop.

Frame Painting Preparation

The amount of preparation work you've got to do before painting that frame depends on the frame itself and just how far you're going to go with the "spit polish" of the frame rails and cross-members. Most reproduction frames from quality manufacturers are relatively easy to finish and paint because the rails and cross-members are new and all the welds are very, very neat.

If, however, your frame was built 50-some years ago, it's going to take just a little more in the way of TLC to get it ready for paint. Rust, the arch enemy of hot-rodders and restorers everywhere, is the most offensive culprit. The two best ways to deal with rust are by sand-

A close inspection reveals areas like this one where rust pits mar the frame rail.

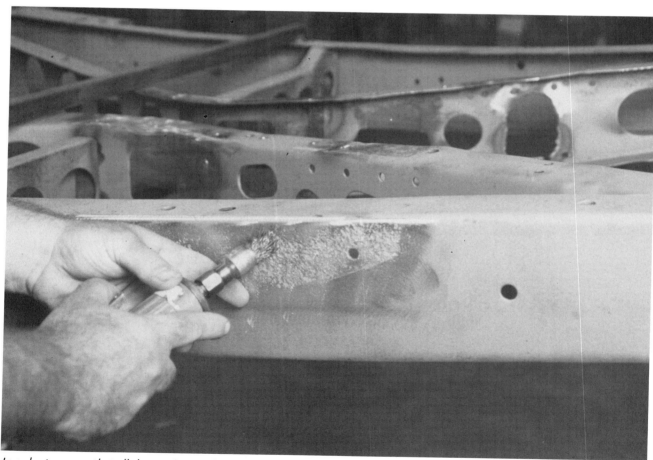

In order to ensure that all the rust is gone from the pits, Steve uses a small wire brush on the end of an air drill to clean up the pitted area.

blasting or dip stripping (more on stripping processes can be found in chapter 4).

While sandblasting doesn't work well on bodies because of the heat and abrasion, there's nothing wrong with having your frame sandblasted at a commercial sandblasting operation. Be sure the operators do a good job and get into all the nooks and crannies as best they can. The advantage of sandblasting is the relatively low cost and the fact that sandblasting companies can be found in nearly all parts of the country. The disadvantage is the inability of the sand media to get into blind corners or the areas where the X-member is riveted to the frame rails.

More expensive, and more thorough, is dip stripping to remove rust. Because frames are relatively large and heavy, they take considerable time to strip, and that stripping isn't exactly cheap. At the time of publication, dipping a complete early style frame cost between $250-$300 (local prices at International Metal Stripping). Fully boxed frames contain a lot more material and cost somewhat more to dip.

Remember that not all frames are square (even the new ones) so you should make sure the frame is level at

Next, Steve grinds the area with a coarse 24 girt pad so the filler that follows will have some good grooves to bite into.

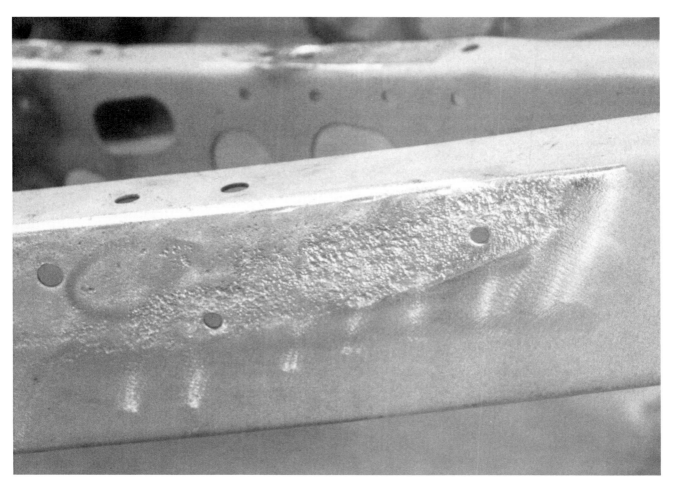

This close up shows the areas after work with the grinder and wire brush.

The first coat of filler is Dura Glass, a waterproof fiberglass-based filler that will not absorb water if it's chipped. After the filler is applied, Steve uses a de-burring tool to clean out the holes in the frame rail.

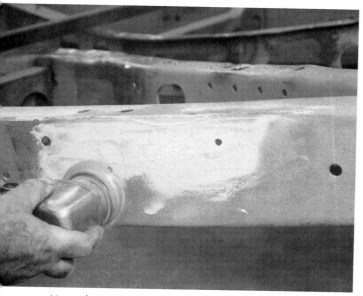

Next, the Dura Glass is sanded and shaped with an 80 grit pad.

all four corners *before* starting in on the finish work. By supporting the frame on three stands—two level stands at the rear and only one in front—with the front stand set in the middle of the front cross-member, the frame is allowed to "float." Any twist in the frame will show up when the level is set across the front of the frame. Be sure to make crisscross measurements of the frame as well (much of this is covered in detail in the book, *Boyd Coddington's How to Build A Hot Rod Chassis*).

Making the Welds Disappear

If a simple paint job for the chassis isn't good enough, then you're going to want to mold all those welds. By carefully molding the welds, the frame becomes one seamless piece that appears to have come out of a mold. Careful finish and paint work will result in a chassis that has the same great looks and finish as the car's body.

Materials

The filler you use to smooth the welds and rough areas depends on personal taste. Some builders like to use a two-part fiberglass-based product like Dura Glass be-

The second coat of filler is a conventional two-part body filler applied in a relatively thin coat.

cause it's more durable and won't absorb moisture if it's chipped. Others use a standard two-part body filler, or body filler over a first coat of Dura Glass.

Because the frame lives in a less than ideal environment, the paint you use needs to be the best that's available. Primer should be a good two-part material. If you're priming a chassis that still has some rust pits, you might want to use a zinc chromate primer (available from Dupont or House of Kolor, among others), as they have better rust inhibiting qualities.

The finish paint you use on the frame should be a good catalyzed urethane. Though the urethanes are more toxic than a straight enamel or acrylic lacquer, the outstanding durability of urethane makes it a good product for the chassis (but remember that using urethanes requires extra caution and safety measures).

Powder paint is a highly durable product—more durable and with a better bond than urethane. Powder coating an entire frame might be tough, but you can have components, such as A-frames and wheels that get an extra load of abuse, powder coated to match the rest of the chassis.

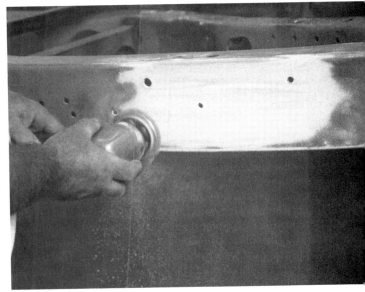

After it sets up, the body filler is sanded with an 80 grit pad on the D-A sander.

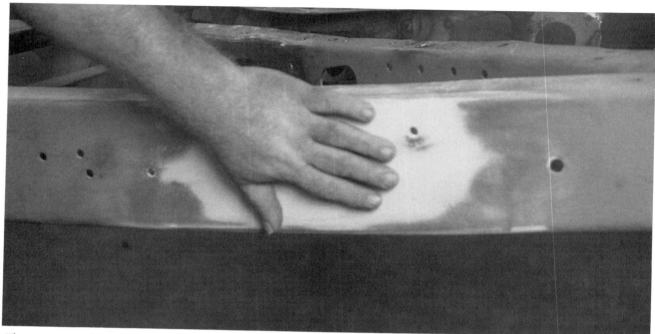

The next step is block sanding with 150 grit paper. A body man's best tool is the palm of his or her hand. Here Steve judges the frame rail as pretty good—some builders would now apply primer-surfacer and finish the frame to the same degree as the body.

A close look at the frame reveals little dings and dents like this along the side rail.

Repair of an old frame requires old-fashioned repair techniques,
like a large crescent wrench and an even larger hammer.

Application of Materials

Whichever filler you use, be sure the preparation is
thorough. Most builders put the filler on over bare steel
(instead of over a two-part primer) and stress the importance of grinding the area to be filled with a 24 grit pad
to leave some "tooth" for the filler to grab onto. Tom
Rad from Twin Town Street Rods feels that, "When the
filler chips on the frame, it's usually because they tried to
apply it over 80 grit scratches. Filler really needs the deep-
er scratches of a 24 grit pad to stick good."

When you're finishing and filling a weld, it's often
tempting to knock off most of the rough weld bead before applying filler. Though this is tempting, it's not a
good idea. You don't know how far that weld pene-
trates—and how much the strength of the weld is com-
promised when you grind off part of the bead. It's far
better to simply rough the area with a 36 or 24 grit pad,
and then use a little extra filler to make the bead disap-
pear.

When it comes to mixing and applying filler, PPG
and some other paint manufacturers feel that the filler
should be applied over a two-part primer. If you choose
to go this route, check with the paint supply store where
you buy all the materials to be sure they approve. Most

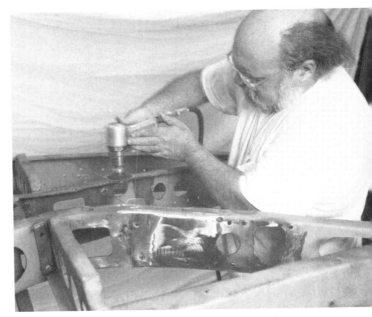

Along with repairs to rusty areas, Steve cleans up the cross-
member where it's been modified to accept the modern Turbo
350 transmission.

143

A frame rotisserie makes the job of grinding hard-to-reach areas much easier.

Before finishing with the frame, Steve fills and sands a few more areas and then prepares the frame for a good coat of primer. The primer Steve uses is a DP product from PPG—a two-part primer that will stick very well to the frame and make a good base for the catalyzed urethane paint to follow.

primers, even good two-part primers, adhere better if the bare steel is treated with a metal prep agent first.

Finishing the filler is done much the same as you would if the filler were applied to a fender or door. Two coats usually suffice, with a third (or some two-part spot putty) for problem areas. Usually the first coat is sanded with a D-A sander equipped with a 36 grit pad. After allowing the second coat of filler to set up, 80 or 100 grit is generally used. And after the optional third coat (or spot putty), it's time for primer-surfacer. How far you go and how careful you are in the final stages of finishing will depend on exactly how particular you (or the judges) are going to be about the finish on the frame.

Hands On: Finishing a Frame at Pete and Jake's

During a recent trip to Kansas City, Missouri, I was able to follow along as Steve Pierce prepared and painted a '41 Ford frame in the Pete and Jake's shop.

The Ford frame wasn't exactly a thing of beauty as it sat on the jigs in the shop. Steve's goal was to take this somewhat beat-up old frame and make it a good-looking foundation for a modern street rod—stopping well short of the full molding treatment. If you plan to build a

The finished frame is now ready for final paint. How far you take a frame in terms of finish and molding is up to you, the procedures are the same, it's just a matter of how much work you want to do.

show frame, read along anyway as the procedures are all the same.

The first step was sandblasting the frame, followed by a good inspection to see if the rust had weakened the frame enough to warrant reinforcing or repair. Steve determined that the frame was sound, and started by identifying areas that he wanted to fill and smooth. Any area that would get filler was wire brushed with an attachment on the end of an electric drill to be sure all the rust was removed from the pits in the metal.

Before starting in with filler, Steve went over the frame with some old-fashioned tools. Kinks in the rails were smoothed out with hammer and dolly or with a large crescent wrench. Rough areas, where metal had been removed to clear the transmission housing, for example, were smoothed out with a small grinder. Once the frame was clean enough and all excess baggage and brackets were removed, Steve could apply the first coat of filler.

Before applying the filler, Steve used a grinder and 24 grit pad to rough up the areas to be filled. For the first coat of filler, Steve used Dura Glass. After the Dura Glass set up, Steve sanded it with a D-A sander and 80 grit

Before painting the engine, Jeff cleans it first with soap and water, followed by wax and grease remover—you can't get 'em too clean.

145

The next step is masking off all the ports, timing chain, and rockers, a job made easier with some wide masking tape.

pad. For the second coat, Steve used a conventional plastic body filler product mixed according to the instructions. This second coat was sanded first with 80 grit, again using a D-A sander, and then with a sanding block and 150 grit paper.

Steve's next step was a good coat of two-part primer. If what you want is a more finely finished frame, two coats of primer-surfacer would be next, followed by sealer (or a two-part primer that can be used as a sealer), and then finish paint.

Painting the Engine

Chrome may still be king, but painted parts seem to gain popularity year by year. Maybe it's just an extension of the "Euro-look" that began ten or more years ago when bumpers and trim went from polished to painted. Not only are bumpers going to paint, so are engines and transmissions. Painting an engine isn't a tough thing to do, it just takes a little extra TLC during preparation and the use of the right materials.

Preparation

Preparation is the most important part of any paint job, and it's especially true if what you're painting is an engine. Because they're so dirty, engines need more cleaning than a body panel. If you're painting the engine before assembly, then the first cleaning steps are part of the overhaul process. But you need more than just a good solvent cleaning of the block, heads and other components. After you've got all the crud washed off, go over the parts with soap and water (dish washing soap and hot water make a good grease-cutting combination), followed by wax and grease remover.

A series of small brushes will make it easier to get down into the crevices and creases. Be patient and thorough; if it isn't clean, the paint just won't stick. If you intend to grind the lumps off the block, do it as soon as the block is disassembled. The fine grinding dust created by the grinding will find its way inside the engine, no matter how careful you are with the masking tape. Rather than try to seal the engine from the dust, why not

After applying the tape, Jeff cuts it to fit each port with a razor blade.

create the dust during a phase of rebuilding where it doesn't make any difference?

The most visible part of most engines is the intake manifold. Even if you don't intend to clean up the block with the grinding disc, you might want to polish (or have polished) the manifold before painting just so it has a nice shine after the paint job.

Paint It!—Materials

Nearly any paint will stick to a nice clean engine, but not all those paint products have the same longevity. Most auto parts stores have engine enamel in a bright rack. Known under a variety of brand names, these paints are designed to withstand higher than normal temperatures. Though these paints work fine, a better product is a catalyzed urethane. Urethane works well on engines for most of the same reasons it works so well on frames. The durability of urethane is unmatched by anything except powder-painting.

The primer you use on engine parts should be a two-part primer due to its superior bonding abilities and great durability. Don't think you can only spray a straight color on the engine. People have successfully used basecoat-clearcoat systems and candy and pearl paints

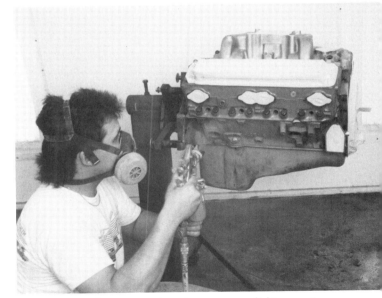

The first coat of two-part primer is put on very light, so as to avoid fish-eyes. It's also important to spray from different angles so the paint gets into all the little low spots on the engine.

on their engine and transmissions as well. Use a few chrome or polished pieces as accents and build a really bright package. Once again, you're limited only by your imagination.

Hands On: Painting an Engine at Twin Town

The engine being painted in the accompanying photos is the proverbial small-block. As always, the first step is cleaning. In spite of the fact that the engine was basically clean (it was recently assembled), Jeff starts with soap and water, followed by wax and grease remover. Next comes the masking operation. Wide tape makes it easier to cover things like exhaust port openings and the timing cover. When all the little nooks and crannies are clean to his satisfaction, Jeff applies the first coat of primer.

Next Jeff mixes up a small amount of blue pearl flakes with some urethane clear—he mixes so little pearl into the clear that the paint on the stir stick shows almost no color.

After applying two coats of primer, Jeff puts on two coats of aqua urethane (a basecoat product from PPG).

The primer Jeff uses is DP 50, a gray catalyzed primer from PPG. Jeff puts the first coat on very light, to minimize the chances of "fish eyes." Jeff explains that, "No matter how careful you are with cleaning, there may still be a slight oily film on the engine—and the oil will cause the paint to fish-eye. So I've learned to use a mist coat for the first coat of primer because it's much less likely to fish-eye. Then I wait for that first coat to flash before I put on a heavier second coat of primer."

Jeff applies the aqua (the paint is Deltron, a catalyzed urethane from PPG) in two coats, allowing the paint to flash per the instructions between coats. When applying both primer and color, Jeff takes care to spray from all angles, so paint is sure to find its way into all the convoluted shapes of the intake manifold and engine block.

After the second coat of color has flashed for 20 minutes, Jeff applies the first of three clearcoats modified with modest amounts of pearl flakes.

Jeff agrees with Doug Thompson that a greater pearl effect is gained by mixing less pearl with the clear and applying more coats. In the case of our engine, three coats

Following the two coats of aqua, Jeff applies two coats of clear-tinted with pearl, and then one final clearcoat.

This is the elaborate frame for the '48 Ford seen in chapter 6. The rails and tubes have been molded and then painted with three coats of the red Concept from PPG—then color-sanded and buffed in the most visible areas.

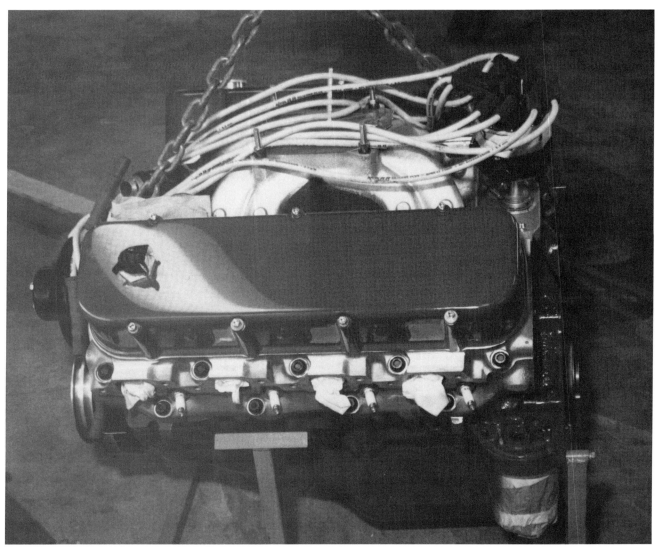

The big-block for the same coupe was painted in the same red used for the body and frame. The valve covers were painted in two stages with color sanding between the two applications, and the full color sand and polish treatment after the last application.

of clear with modest amounts of pearl provide the subtle effect that Jeff was after. Before finishing, Jeff applies one straight clearcoat as the final step in the engine painting process.

Finally

Remember that preparation is the most important part of any painting operation. Given the fact that frames and engines are often dirty, greasy, *and* rusty, the need for thorough pre-paint cleaning is especially true with engines.

When painting frames and engines, it's important to get the metal as clean and rust-free as possible. And since these components live in a very hostile environment after they've been painted, it's important to pay particular attention to the paint materials you use.

But with a little extra care and the correct choice in paint materials you can have a frame or engine that looks as good as you want it to. Flat black or candy orange—it's all up to you.

Appendix

Sources

Binks
Bill Mott
Griggs Midway Building
1821 University Avenue
St. Paul, MN 55104

B.T. Design
Brian Truesdell
937 Smith Avenue South
St. Paul, MN 55118

International Metal Stripping
3520 International Drive
St. Paul, MN 55110
Paint stripping

Graco/Croix Air
c/o American Turbines, Inc.
3274 Highway 61
White Bear Lake, MN 55110

Tim Whelan
HVLP equipment

Krazy Kolors
Attn: Lenny Schwartz
453 W. Seventh Street
St. Paul, MN 55102
Pinstriping

House of Kolor
Jon Kosmoski
2521 27th Avenue S.
Minneapolis, MN 55406
Custom paint supplies

Mattson Spray Equipment
230 W. Coleman Street
Rice Lake, WI 54868
Spray guns and equipment

PPG Finishes
19699 Progress Drive
Strongsville, OH 44136
Paints and related products

Strip Right
7901 Beech Street N.E.
Fridley, MN 55432
Plastic blasting

Twin Town Street Rods
209 Ryan Drive
St. Paul, MN 55117
Paint jobs

Unique Body and Paint
612/784-3159
9195 N.E. Davenport Street
Blaine, MN 55434
Paint jobs

Index